HEROES OF THE WOMEN'S SUFFRAGE MOVEMENT

CHAMPIONS FOR WOMEN'S RIGHTS

MATILDA JOSLYN GAGE, JULIA WARD HOWE, LUCRETIA MOTT, AND LUCY STONE

LYNN BARBER

In loving memory of Mary Church and Celia Electa Barber

Published in 2017 by Enslow Publishing, LLC.
101 W. 23rd Street, Suite 240, New York, NY 10011

Library of Congress Cataloging-in-Publication Data
Names: Barber, Lynn, author.
Title: Champions for women's rights : Matilda Joslyn Gage, Julia Ward Howe, Lucretia Mott, and Lucy Stone / Lynn Barber.
Description: New York, NY : Enslow Publishing, 2017. | Series: Heroes of the women's suffrage movement | Audience: Grade 9 to 12. | Includes bibliographical references and index.
Identifiers: LCCN 2016004684 | ISBN 9780766078918 (library bound)
Subjects: LCSH: Women's rights—United States—Juvenile literature. | Women—Suffrage—United States—Juvenile literature. | Women—Legal status, laws, etc.—United States—Juvenile literature. | Gage, Matilda Joslyn, 1826-1898. | Howe, Julia Ward, 1819-1910. | Mott, Lucretia, 1793-1880. | Stone, Lucy, 1818-1893.
Classification: LCC HQ1236.5.U6 B37 2016 | DDC 323.3/40973—dc23
LC record available at http://lccn.loc.gov/2016004684

Printed in the United States of America

CONTENTS

INTRODUCTION
BEFORE SUFFRAGE..4

CHAPTER ONE
MATILDA JOSLYN GAGE..20

CHAPTER TWO
JULIA WARD HOWE...42

CHAPTER THREE
LUCRETIA COFFIN MOTT...63

CHAPTER FOUR
LUCY STONE..87

CHAPTER FIVE
THE LEGACY..110

CHAPTER NOTES..116

GLOSSARY...120

FURTHER READING...122

INDEX..124

BEFORE SUFFRAGE

In the 1800s, life was demanding and hard for American women, and it was often cruel. The woman of the house was expected to do just about everything related to the domestic life of the family. She would get up early—often before dawn—and get a fire started in the fireplace or stove. That began a day of preparing meals, tending children, scrubbing floors, washing clothes, working in her garden, feeding chickens, milking cows, sewing, mending, preserving food, and caring for anyone who was sick, including herself. It was true that "a woman's work was never done."

She was also expected to be obedient, meek, and submissive to her husband or father. She was viewed as inferior to a man—mentally, physically, and even morally. Women were often called "the Daughters of Eve," indicating that they were basically sinful and were responsible for leading men into sin.

If a woman did not do as her husband told her, or if what she did displeased him, he was well within his legal rights to beat her. The

PUNCH, OR THE LONDON CHARIVARI.—MAY 30, 1874.

" WOMAN'S WRONGS."

BRUTAL HUSBAND. "AH! YOU'D BETTER GO SNIVELLIN' TO THE 'OUSE O' COMMONS, *YOU* HAD! MUCH THEY'RE LIKELY TO DO FOR YER! YAH! READ THAT!"

"Mr. DISRAELI.—There can be but one feeling in the House on the subject of these dastardly attacks—not upon the weaker but the fairer sex. (*A laugh.*) I am sure the House shares the indignation of my hon. friend who will, I hope, consider he has secured the object he had in view by raising the question. * * * Assuring my hon. friend that Her Majesty's Government will not lose sight of the question, I must ask him not to press his Motion further on the present occasion."—*Parliamentary Report, Monday, May 18.*

This British newspaper illustration depicts an all too common scenario in nineteenth-century England and the United States. Men could take out their aggression on their wives with no repercussions.

ANNE HUTCHINSON (1591–1643)

Anne Hutchinson was one of the earliest women religious leaders in colonial America. She was a Puritan woman who disagreed about church doctrine and publicly voiced that disagreement. She was a respected member of the Massachusetts Bay Colony and was a skilled herbalist, midwife, and healer. She had many friends and followers because of her work in the community. She was brought to trial not only for her disagreement with religious doctrine, but for speaking out publicly—an unacceptable behavior for a woman. She believed she had the right to have an opinion and to voice that opinion, even though she was a woman. The religious leaders of the Massachusetts Bay Colony brought her to trial and convicted her. She was banished from the colony and excommunicated from her religion.

phrase "rule of thumb" came from legal decisions that basically said a man was allowed to beat his wife with a rod no larger than his thumb. A woman could not bring her husband to trial for physical abuse such as this since she was not regarded as a separate person from her husband. It was generally accepted by the public that a man had a right to punish his wife in any way he wished. Even the church and the clergy would have regarded this as acceptable, even admirable. It was, after all, the husband's responsibility to discipline his wife since she was considered childlike and without a mind of her own.

What was life like for single women? In the 1820s and 1830s, the textile industry had developed in New England and young, single women found work at these factories—for very low wages, working very long days. But this work enabled them to help their families or to earn money to bring into

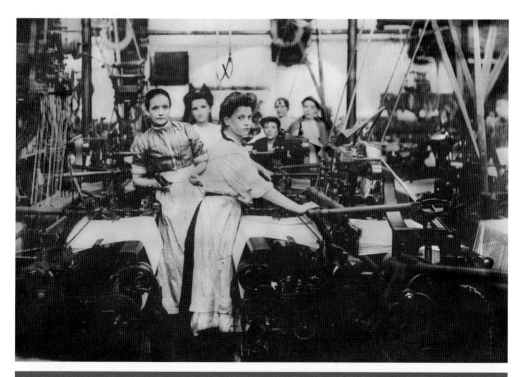

The Industrial Revolution brought opportunities for young single women. Working in textile factories gave them financial independence that married women did not enjoy.

a future marriage. However, most did stop working and got married after a few years.

Single women were in some ways better off. They had some rights as individuals, since they were not under the control of a husband. They could earn money, and they could receive an inheritance. But once a woman married, everything she owned became her husband's. He could take from her everything she inherited and everything she might earn, however small.

WOMEN'S RIGHTS?

A woman's rights were extremely limited in terms of educational opportunity, legal rights, earning power, and political and societal influence—and even in her ability to control what happened to her own body. Even how she dressed was strictly controlled. Most women wore a corset around the waist and upper body. The corset had rigid "stays," which were often made of whalebone. These were extremely uncomfortable and limited a woman's movement. The corset also constricted her lungs and other internal organs, often causing physical damage and health issues. It also made women faint, as they could not breathe easily. Fainting reinforced the notion that women were weak, feeble creatures who were always ill and not strong. Dresses were very long and swept the ground, bringing dirt and germs from the streets into the house. Petticoats under the dresses weighed up to 12 pounds (5.4 kilograms)! These dresses were heavy and tiring for women to wear, and the length of the dress made walking difficult and unsafe.

Almost all women wore long hair that took time and skill to clean and arrange. A woman's hair was also referred to as "her crowning glory" in the Bible, and therefore long hair was prized, even though it was time consuming and impractical for women who were required to perform so much physical labor.

Women's clothing was restrictive, like the rest of their lives. Their long skirts and suffocating corsets added to their suffering.

Women had limited opportunities to be outside the home. Their social life consisted of meeting with other women in sewing circles or other home-related gatherings and going to church. Otherwise, women stayed at home because a woman's place was in the home.

A married woman could not own property, could not make a legal contract, could not sue or be sued, could not sit on a jury, and could not vote. A wife could only make a legal will if her husband agreed with what it said and signed off on it. A woman's husband was literally her "lord and master." He controlled her and her children in every way. She could not stop him if he chose to beat or abuse her children. He could decide to send a child away to learn a skill from a blacksmith, or a barrel maker, or a leather tanner, or any other trade, without his wife's permission. He could send a child away from the house if that child displeased him, and the mother could not stop him. If the husband drank or gambled and lost all his income, the family

EARLY VOTING RIGHTS

Most state constitutions specifically denied women the right to vote. But in 1783, all residents of New Jersey "worth fifty pounds proclamation money" could vote. By 1800, local politicians complained that women voting would lead to having a legislature "filled with petticoats" because women had voted in large numbers for a certain county representative. Since married women could not have money independent of their husbands, their status as voters was eliminated.[1]

could become destitute, and the wife would have no legal rights to deal with this situation.

Even when the husband died, he continued to have absolute power over his wife and children. He could will his children to someone other than their mother, and she would have no way to stop it. Often, his widow could continue to live in her house only for a brief time after his death without paying rent and could have the use of only one-third of her deceased husband's land and properties while she lived.[2]

WHAT COULD WOMEN DO?

Marriage was considered the only true "career" for women. If a woman did not marry by the time she reached a certain age—and that age could be as young as her mid-twenties—she was known as a spinster. This was considered a sad state for a woman because she had not fulfilled her role as a woman: to be a wife and a mother. A spinster did not have her own household to run or her own children. She would have had little opportunity for work other than caring for aging parents or ailing relatives.

While there were few opportunities to work outside of the home, women were more than occupied by the heavy work that had to be done at home. Most of America was rural at that time, and there was no running water, central heating, or indoor plumbing to be had by even the wealthiest

Carrying on the traditions of colonial women, American women in the nineteenth century filled their days with exhausting physical work. They were responsible for everything related to the home and family, with none of the conveniences we take for granted today.

households. Most women lived lives filled with exhausting and unending physical labor. Water had to be brought in from an outside well. Then it had to be heated for cleaning, cooking, and bathing. A fire would have been burning all the time, even on the hottest days of summer.

A woman might have sold eggs, cheese, butter, or some other produce or taken in sewing to bring in some additional income to the household, but that money was always controlled by the husband.

In addition to backbreaking work, women were responsible for the early education and religious training of their children. With limited education themselves, most women could at best read the Bible and manage basic household accounts. Books would not have been available except in a very affluent household.

For a woman in a wealthy household, life might have been somewhat easier. There might have been servants to help with some of the heavy work. A woman in this setting might have had an opportunity for some kind of higher learning, but the focus of any education would have been to make her a more desirable wife. She would have learned to draw, sing, and paint, and perhaps play a musical instrument, embroider cushions, or create needlepoint. But there her education would have stopped. It would not have been a "classical" education such as men received, which included the study of Greek and Roman literature, geometry, history, philosophy, archaeology, and other related subjects. That would have been frowned on as a waste of time and money, as no woman would be actually using that knowledge. Also, it might discourage a husband who did not want a wife who was more educated than he. Sons were educated, since they were expected to make their way in the world, but women—no matter how bright and eager to learn— were not considered worthy of education.

WOMEN'S GROUPS AND EDUCATIONAL PROGRESS

A step forward in women's education occurred with the founding of the Troy Female Seminary by Emma Willard in 1821. This was a school that offered an educational opportunity for women that was similar to the classical education pro- vided to men. It enabled women to begin careers as teachers—the first real profession occupied by women—even if they were paid far less than men for their work. Churches were places where women could meet together, discuss, plan, and ultimately take action on important social issues. Religion was very important to most women, and there was intense interest in making society better. Helping widows and orphans, families that had been aban- doned by the male head of the household, or the sick and elderly were all very important activities for women. They formed groups and societies to address these problems in their communities.

Women in the nineteenth and early twentieth centuries joined temperance societies to advocate for alcohol abstinence.

One of the issues that moved women's groups to action was temperance. Temperance, or promising to drink alcohol, was a big concern for many women. Since women had no legal recourse if their husbands drank away the family income, the problem of alcohol abuse by the head of the household could be extremely damaging to a family. Women's groups advocated for general abstinence from alcohol, but the movement finally won the legal prohibition of alcohol. Many women involved with the temperance movement were also suffragists, believing that if women had the vote, they could create a more virtuous society.

WHAT ABOUT ENSLAVED WOMEN, NATIVE AMERICAN WOMEN, AND FREE BLACK WOMEN?

There were other women in America who experienced very different lives, such as enslaved women, free black women, and Native American women. In the Iroquois Nation of upstate New York, women were respected in their tribes and clans. They were considered the equals of men in terms of governing and maintaining the life and culture of their society. The Iroquois are a matrilineal culture, which means that a person's ancestry is traced through the mother's side of the family. Women were also responsible for selecting and overseeing the male tribal leaders and for managing the land of the tribe, as well as performing household duties such as cooking and caring for children.

Many women in the free black population were active in women's circles and other church groups, and they were eager to find opportunity for their children and families in an environment often openly hostile to them. Education for their children was a strong concern for these women. While some schools were founded specifically for African American children, they were few, and females were the last to receive educational benefits.

Even more desperate was the condition of enslaved African American women. They were property and could be treated in any way the master chose. They could be sold or their children could be sold. Teaching an enslaved child to write was a crime in the South. Female slaves were vulnerable to overwork and abuse of all kinds, particularly by their owners. Suffrage and other freedoms were far beyond the harsh realities of their lives.

PRUDENCE CRANDALL (1803–1890)

Quaker educator Prudence Crandall fought valiantly against the bias against educating young black females. Crandall ran a school for affluent young ladies near Hartford, Connecticut, in the 1830s. She was asked to include a young black girl in her classes, and she accepted. Her white pupils and their families were outraged and demanded that she oust the black student. She refused and closed her school, opening it again with the mission of educating more young black females. She faced violence and hostility, including being put under arrest. She and her students continued, supported by the abolitionist cause, until her house and school were attacked and nearly destroyed by a mob.

THE RISE OF THE ABOLITION MOVEMENT AND THE FIGHT FOR WOMEN'S SUFFRAGE

The terrible suffering caused by slavery in America awoke the conscience of many people. Some took action and opposed slavery. They were called abolitionists, and their goal was to end the institution of slavery and to free those who were enslaved. While the abolition movement was at work in both the North and the South, it was least influential in the southern states, where the institution of slavery was a powerful economic force.

Among the most courageous advocates for abolition in the South were two sisters, Angelina and Sarah Grimké. Daughters of a wealthy South Carolina slave owner, the sisters broke with their family and began speaking against slavery. First they spoke only to women, as it was then considered improper for women to speak to a mixed group of men and women. In that time, women were not supposed to speak publicly at all. They spoke only in private homes. The Grimké sisters experienced so many barriers to their work simply because they were women, and they quickly became impassioned advocates for women's rights as well as abolition.

The same realization that freedom for slaves and the freedom of women were interconnected occurred to many women who were to become leaders in the suffrage movement, including the four amazing women suffragists described in this book: Matilda Joslyn Gage, Julia Ward Howe, Lucretia Mott, and Lucy Stone.

All four of these women suffragists were extraordinary women in their time—and if they were transported to modern times, they would be just as extraordinary. They were tireless, they were courageous, and they were dedicated to advocating for women's rights and suffrage. If they were here now, they would be advocating for equal pay for equal work; more opportunities for higher education; quality health care for women; more women in science, math, and technology careers; more women in judicial and legislative roles; and women's rights and equality all over the world.

Angelina Grimké and her sister Sarah fought to end slavery after witnessing its horrors on their family plantation.

MATILDA JOSLYN GAGE

Matilda Electa Joslyn was born in 1826 in Cicero, New York. Both her parents, Dr. Hezekiah Joslyn and his wife, Helen Leslie, were active in reformist causes including abolition. Matilda Joslyn's home was a stop on the Underground Railroad. She remembered going as a child to hear Abby Kelley speak about the cruelties that were inflicted on male and female slaves. These experiences created in her a hatred for the oppression of any human being.

Everything around her was preparing her to be the brilliant and radical suffrage activist she would become. From her youngest days, her father was eager to provide his only child with a quality education. He taught her mathematics, physiology, and Greek. The house was filled with her parents' friends, who were knowledgeable in philosophy, theology, and the sciences. She was particularly

Matilda Joslyn Gage's eloquent and passionate writings helped further the women's suffrage movement. Gage began her activism in the antislavery movement before turning her talents to the rights of women.

ULTRA ABOLITIONIST AND SUFFRAGIST ABBY KELLEY FOSTER (1811–1887)

Abigail (Abby) Kelley Foster grew up in a Quaker family and became a lecturer for William Lloyd Garrison's American Anti-Slavery Society. She later married fellow abolitionist and lecturer Stephen Foster, and together they continued to work for equal rights for women. Kelley also worked with abolitionists such as Angelina Grimké. She became an "ultra"–working for not only abolition, but also for full rights for blacks in society and in politics. She was influenced by Garrison to adopt a philosophy of "nonresistance," which not only opposed war but also any kind of governmental authority such as requiring that a person serve on a jury or join the military. Along with Lucy Stone and other suffragists, she refused to pay taxes on her home. Like Lucy Stone, she also supported the Fifteenth Amendment, which was opposed by Susan B. Anthony and Elizabeth Cady Stanton.

interested in the study of theology. Her father felt
that she needed a more formalized education,
so he sent her to the Clinton New York Liberal
Institute, where she studied until she was eighteen.

ABOLITION ACTIVITIES

In 1844, she married Henry H. Gage, who was also an abolitionist, and they moved to Syracuse, New York, and then to the small town of Fayetteville near Syracuse. The couple had four children who survived to adulthood. Together, Matilda and Henry opened their Fayetteville home to the Underground Railroad. Gage's oldest daughter said that one of her "earliest remembrances is that of a black man on his knees before her mother, thanking her for a chance of life and liberty."[1]

In offering safety to a runaway slave, the Gages put themselves at risk of arrest and imprisonment for breaking the Fugitive Slave Act. But Gage did more than this. She was the only person in Fayetteville to sign a statement saying that she would give aid to any slave who was seeking to gain his or her liberty, and for that reason she was under constant watch by the local authorities.[2] Gage continued to shelter runaway slaves until the Civil War was over. The Gage home became a meeting place for antislavery discussion and planning and was visited by those who worked for abolition, temperance, and women's suffrage, including Susan B. Anthony, Elizabeth Cady Stanton, Gerrit Smith, and Charles Sumner.

Gage's husband also worked with people in the central New York area to advocate against slavery's being extended into new territories in the western

United States, such as Kansas. Gage also raised funds to supply a local regiment with equipment and arms to fight for the Union.

Gage found other antislavery supporters at the Fayetteville Baptist Church, which, before she arrived in Fayetteville, had experienced great division over the issue of slavery. But by the time Gage settled there, the church was a center of antislavery sentiment.

ACTIVISM FOR WOMEN'S RIGHTS

Gage attended the Third Women's Rights National Convention in Syracuse in 1852. Both she and Susan B. Anthony made their first public speeches at this convention. Gage was shaking uncontrollably. She had never spoken in public before. She was twenty-six years old and the youngest speaker at the convention. Observers commented that she spoke so softly the audience could hardly hear her.[3] But she would be remembered for far more important reasons in the coming years. Her speech concentrated on the many achievements of women through history and the need for women to break through the legal and economic limitations forced on them by society. She returned again and again to the similarity between the oppression of women and the institution of slavery. She believed that both these social ills came from the same patriarchal values. Her words so moved the audience that

Gage worked closely with one of the women's movement's notable leaders, Susan B. Anthony *(above)*. Along with Elizabeth Cady Stanton, the two women founded the National Woman Suffrage Association.

her remarks were printed and circulated to the public to gain more support for women's suffrage. It was just four years after the regional Women's Convention in Seneca Falls, NY.

In 1869, Anthony, Stanton, and Gage were the cofounders of the National Woman Suffrage Association (NWSA). The three suffragists founded this organization because they felt that existing suffrage groups were not advocating strongly enough for women's rights and that it was important to address issues other than getting the vote for women. Gage believed that the vote would not automatically solve the oppression of women in America.

When Susan B. Anthony successfully cast her vote in the 1872 presidential election and was then arrested for it, Matilda Gage was there to support her. She was the only suffragist who came forward to help Anthony. Gage herself had tried to vote in 1871 but had been denied. Gage spoke on behalf of Anthony and stayed with her during the trial.

In 1875, Gage went to Washington, DC, to testify on behalf of a women's suffrage bill. The bill did not pass. Gage was furious. In January of 1876, Gage was attending an NWSA convention held in Washington, DC, and sent a protest to fellow NWSA members saying that women should not join in celebrating the upcoming centennial (the one-hundredth anniversary of the beginning of the nation) because the nation was not a democracy but an unequal and unfair state in which men held all political and economic power.[4]

Government officials did not like hearing this kind of accusation, and so they went to the convention to close it down. Gage stood up to the police, saying she would not end the convention and that if she was arrested she would continue to lead the convention in jail.[5]

She believed that disrespect for women was very deeply ingrained in nineteeth-century American culture and in many of the institutions that were pillars of that culture. Chief among them was the Christian church, which, Gage thought, often presented women in a negative light. She felt that the accomplishments of women had been left out of history—and the Bible—and she sought to highlight some of those

Elizabeth Cady Stanton wrote *The Woman's Bible* with the help of an esteemed reviewing committee, including Matilda Gage.

accomplishments in her pamphlets "Woman as Inventor" (1870), "Woman's Rights Catechism" (1871), and "Who Planned the Tennessee Campaign of 1862?" (1880). Gage documented, as noted on the Gage Foundation website, unrecognized accomplishments such as Catherine Littlefield Greene's invention of the cotton gin, wrongly attributed to Eli Whitney.[6]

Susan B. Anthony, Elizabeth Cady Stanton, and Gage together were involved in leading the NWSA for more than twenty years. Gage was an excellent writer and worked as a correspondent to many newspapers all over the nation, writing about suffrage and women's issues. She and Stanton wrote many of the policies for the NWSA. Gage also founded the *National Citizen and Ballot Box*, the newspaper of the NWSA. This paper was designed to educate and inspire action for women's rights, and it was published from her home in Fayetteville.

Gage also collaborated with Stanton and Anthony on writing and editing the multivolume *History of Woman Suffrage*, as well as the Declaration of the Rights of Women. She and Stanton also worked together on writing a revised version of the Bible, which was to be called *The Woman's Bible*. Gage had done considerable research on translating the Bible.

Gage had provided organizing leadership to both the Virginia and the New York Woman Suffrage associations. The New York association had won the right for women in New York to vote for—and run in—school elections. Gage organized Fayetteville women to vote, and she was the first one in line to vote. The voters, including women now, elected an all-woman slate. In 1893—thirteen years after the election!—Gage was brought to court in a test case to determine the constitutionality of the New York law that gave women the right to vote in school elections. She lost. Women in New York now had no opportunity to vote at the state or federal level.[7]

In 1890, she left the NWSA and formed a new organization called the Women's National Liberal Union (WNLU). This organization's purpose was to advocate for women's suffrage and separation of church and state, and to oppose the demeaning or belittling of women, whether in writing, in church sermons, or in political speeches. Stanton and Anthony were angry at her for leaving the NWSA, and they publicly condemned her for doing so. They believed Gage had gone too far in her radical politics, and they did not want to alienate the conservative, religious faction of the suffrage movement.

They purposely removed the work that Gage had done for women's suffrage from the *History of Woman Suffrage*. This omission meant that Gage would not get serious attention from scholars and historians for many decades to come.

FRANCES WILLARD, TEMPERANCE LEADER (1839–1898)

Willard was active in reforms for education, temperance, and women's rights. She worked for the adoption of the Eighteenth (prohibition) and Nineteenth (vote for women) Amendments to the US Constitution. Willard was president of the WCTU from 1879 to her death in 1898. She encouraged her membership to engage in any activity that would move the temperance movement forward. Her work also led to strong antirape laws and protections against child abuse. Willard ran into trouble with progressive African American journalist and antilynching crusader Ida B. Wells because the WCTU, trying to court Southern support, had portrayed black males as likely to commit crimes against white women while under the influence of alcohol. Wells also questioned Willard's position on lynching.

THE POWER OF CHURCH AND STATE

Gage was increasingly concerned about the growth of a conservative religious faction in American politics. Their ultimate objective was to establish a

Christian nation, thereby combining religion with the state. To Gage, this would have been a serious blow to the women's rights movement since, in her view, both the state and the Christian church had been responsible for oppressing women for centuries.

One of the reasons Gage left the NWSA was because Stanton and Anthony were pursuing a political alliance with Frances Willard's conservative Woman's Christian Temperance Union (WCTU). At this time, Willard had said that she wanted an amendment to the US Constitution stating that Jesus Christ was the head of the American government.

This repulsed Gage, who believed that the Christian church was founded on the idea that woman was second to man; that Christianity was founded on a myth; that science was constantly proving it to be wrong; that the Christian church had taken woman's freedom to think, reason, and act; and that it was important to free woman from the church's influence.

VIOLENCE AGAINST WOMEN THROUGHOUT THE AGES

Anthony and Stanton continued to attack Gage for her unrelenting criticism of the Christian church, but Gage persisted. In 1893, Gage wrote perhaps her most well-known work, *Woman, Church, and State* (1893). In this book, Gage describes

civilizations in history where women had great freedom and where the "Matriarchate" or "mother rule,"[8]
was the guiding force in society. These civilizations
included ancient Egypt; Roman, Scandinavian, and
Hindu cultures; and the Iroquois Nation in the New
World. It was in these societies, Gage states, that
the concept of "inherent rights," or the rights that
every human being has just because he or she is
a human being, was conceived. She describes the
rise of the "Patriarchate," or rule by the male as
head of family or group, which women in western
Europe began to experience in about 500 CE.
Laws were made so that women could no longer
inherit a throne or a fiefdom (a large area of land
that was ruled over by a lord). Therefore, a female
heir could no longer rule over lands and people.
That would now go to the nearest male relative.

Gage also describes the terrible period of witch
burning in early medieval Europe. She points out
that the vast majority of those who were put to
death as witches were women and that the property of these women was often forfeited (or turned
over) to the very people or institutions that were
executing them.

"Wise women" who knew how to use plants
and herbs to heal, medicate, and help reduce
the pain of childbirth were often regarded as
evil by the church because the pain of childbirth
was thought to be "punishment" for Eve and her
descendants for eating the "forbidden fruit" (the

One chapter in the long history of misogyny was the practice of killing women who were accused of being witches. Women who were different or perceived as threatening were often accused and then drowned or burned at the stake.

apple). The terror and torture used against women during the time of witch burning were effective tactics in suppressing women's intellectual growth and expression.[9] Gage was outraged about these crimes not only because they were committed against innocent women but because some of these women may have had knowledge of the woman-centered spirituality that existed before the patriarchal power structure began to subordinate women. Gage also commented on the abuse of elderly women, not only during the days of the witch burnings, but in the current age. Gage felt that these misogynistic (woman-hating) attitudes were still powerful in the Christian church of that day, and she feared the combined power of church and state would prevent women from obtaining their rights.

The WNLU proved successful at first, attracting liberal suffragists and those who believed in separation of church and state, among others, to its first convention. Participants came from thirty-three states.[10] But the organization did not last. After the publication of its first magazine, the *Liberal Thinker*, the organization ran out of funds. Progressives and freethinkers were interested in the organization, but it made powerful enemies, including some in the federal government.

While WNLU's membership thought everyone had the right to believe—or not believe—in religion, not everyone was in agreement with this philosophy. Churches preached sermons against Gage and the WNLU. But Gage persevered in her writing and criticism of the hypocrisy (claiming to believe in one set of values, but behaving in an opposite way) of the Christian church. She stated that the church criticized her for voicing her concerns about the condition of women in society, while failing to speak out against the sexual abuse of women and children. She noted that while the morality of the time did not allow any open discussion of human sexuality, pornography, prostitution, and child abuse were thriving in Victorian society.

THE SKY CARRIER

In contrast to her views about Victorian society, Gage thought highly of the civilization of the Iroquois—or as they preferred to be known, the Haudenosaunee—Confederacy. There were originally five tribes, or nations, who were members of the confederacy: Mohawk, Oneida, Onondaga, Seneca, and Cayuga. Others were added through military victories and adoption.

These tribes were originally located throughout the northeastern United States, but in Gage's life-time, they were primarily concentrated in the Finger Lakes region of New York State. Gage lived in this area all her life. She had studied the Iroquois and knew and admired their culture. Tribal membership was inherited through the mother. Whatever clan (groups within the tribe) the mother was, her children would also be members of that clan. Unlike the white American culture in Gage's time, the children of Iroquois mothers were under her control. If for some reason the mother wished to leave her hus-band, the children were hers without question. She also took all the property she had brought into the marriage. Again, this was just the opposite of what white women in America were experiencing.

Gage had written a series of articles about the Iroquois when she was younger. She was

WE, THE WOMEN OF THE IROQUOIS:

Own the land, the lodge, the children.

Ours is the right of adoption, of life or death;

Ours the right to raise up and depose chiefs;

Ours the right of representation at all councils;

Ours the right to make and abrogate treaties;

Ours the supervision over domestic and foreign policies;

Ours the trusteeship of the tribal property;

Our lives are valued again as high as man's.

SAVAGERY TO "CIVILIZATION"

Drawn by JOSEPH KEPPLER

THE INDIAN WOMEN: We whom you pity as drudges reached centuries ago the goal that you are now nearing

This 1914 political cartoon depicts Iroquois women on a cliff overlooking suffragettes marching, carrying a banner proclaiming "woman suffrage." The ironic caption reflects the elevated position of women in Iroquois society.

impressed with the power that women wielded in the tribes and clans and how they were respected and considered as equals by the men of the tribe. Women had equal decision-making power in matters of war and peace, and no decisions about land could be made without the women's consent.

As white settlers in America began to move west, the Native American tribes were pushed out of their own lands. Sometimes the US government made treaties with them to use their land. But the government often broke those treaties and quickly lost the respect of Native Americans.

Gage spoke out against this unfair treatment of Native Americans in her newspaper, the *National Citizen and Ballot Box*. It seemed very ironic to her that the government was trying to get Native Americans to accept US citizenship and voting rights, when it would not do the same for its African American and female citizens. However, the objective of the government was to get Native American land for white settlers in exchange for promises of citizenship. Gage advocated that Native Americans should have the right to maintain their status as an independent nation.

When Gage visited the Mohawk tribe, she was adopted into the Wolf Clan. She was given the name of "She who holds up the sky." It must have seemed ironic to Gage that shortly before she received this honor, she had been arrested for voting in her own country.[11]

THE WIZARD OF OZ

Despite Gage's intense commitment to women's rights and other causes, she did have a home and family. Gage gave birth to five children but lost her first son in his infancy. Of the remaining four children, Maud was her youngest. She greatly surprised her mother by announcing that she wanted to marry a young, struggling writer named L. Frank Baum (the author of *The Wonderful Wizard of*

GLORIA STEINEM (1934–)

Gloria Steinem is a writer, lecturer, political activist, and feminist organizer. Steinem cofounded *Ms.* magazine, the first American progressive feminist magazine. It covers issues of discrimination against women, political activity to overcome discrimination, and stories of women's political and economic achievements. Steinem helped to found the Women's Action Alliance, a national information center that specialized in nonsexist, multiracial children's education, and the National Women's Political Caucus, a group that continues to work to increase the number of pro-equality women in elected and appointed office at the national and state level. She also cofounded the Women's Media Center in 2004.

Oz). At first, Gage resisted the idea. She told her daughter that this young man was not financially stable and that he could not take care of Maud. But then she realized that she was not being a good example of letting each person make his or her own decisions. Maud had had the opportunity to have a career in law at a time when this was a very uncommon career for a woman.

Gage spent time each year with Maud and her husband. Baum loved and respected her and called her the most gifted and educated woman of her age.[12] His creation of the Land of Oz reflects some of Gage's thinking regarding the benefits of a matriarchate and the elements of a just society.

Gage had suffered ill health, which forced her to give up her activist work. She died at the age of seventy-two at the Baum home in Chicago in 1898. She was cremated—yet another bold act for the time—and has a memorial stone at the Fayetteville Cemetery, inscribed with her own words: "There is a word sweeter than Mother, Home or Heaven. That word is Liberty."[13]

LEGACY

The words on Gage's memorial stone described her philosophy and world view perfectly. Liberty was what she worked for during her entire life, whether it was for the abolition of slavery, the rights of Native Americans, or the rights of women.

She was a visionary, and even today her ideas still create both controversy and inspiration. She believed that women deserved their rights simply because they were human beings, not because their morality was any more virtuous than men's. Her goal was that women should have the vote for themselves, not because of what they might do for others if they had the vote.

Despite her consistent criticism of the Christian church, Gage had a deep, personal spirituality that was connected to the early woman-centered religions of the Matriarchate.

Because Gage was a radical, and because she was largely excluded from the *History of Woman Suffrage*, little was known about her work for some time after her death. In 2000, the Matilda Joslyn Gage Foundation was incorporated with the mission of educating current and future generations about the work of Matilda Joslyn Gage. The foundation purchased Gage's home in Fayetteville, NY, and has opened it to the public as a place to learn more about Gage and her work. The founding director, Sally Roesch Wagner, PhD, is the nation's foremost authority on Gage and is also a biographer of Gage.

Another legacy of Gage is a fascinating research finding on how recognition is given for science research work. The study discovered that there was systematic denial of the contributions of women scientists and that their work was often attributed to male scientists. This effect was described as the "Matilda effect"[14] because Gage had uncovered so many instances of men being credited with inventions actually made by women.

Perhaps the greatest honor paid to Gage was made by the contemporary feminist and women's rights leader Gloria Steinem, who said in an invitation for an event on behalf of the Gage Foundation, "Meet Matilda Joslyn Gage, the woman who was *ahead* of the women who were ahead of their time."[15]

CHAPTER TWO

JULIA WARD HOWE

Julia Ward Howe came from an upper-middle-class background, unlike the other three suffragists described in this book. She was born in New York City in 1819 and was the fourth of seven children. Her father, Samuel Ward III, was a successful Wall Street banker and was very strict about religion. Her mother, Julia, was a published poet. Julia Ward's mother died shortly after giving birth to her seventh child, so the children were left to the care of their aunt Eliza. Despite the loss of her mother, Julia had a happy childhood. While her father was strict, he loved his children and spent time with them. However, his religious beliefs became stricter, and he no longer allowed his children to attend plays or the theater. But Julia was not discouraged. At the age of nine, she wrote and presented a play of her own to her brothers and sisters. She was tutored at home and soon learned

Julia Ward Howe is shown in her later years in this circa 1906 photograph. Howe was a prolific writer of poetry and plays, many of which examined the role of women in society.

to speak French fluently, to read Latin and Italian, to play and sing music, and to write poetry. Julia was very intelligent and very creative. She had a tremendous intellect and was interested in literature, philosophy, religion, and languages, and she seriously pursued them all.

She was eager to learn and had the resources and the opportunity to learn—within reason. Her strict, religiously conservative father forbade her to study anything that he did not approve of. Julia studied with tutors that her father had selected. She never attended a school outside her home

But life was about to change for Julia. Her father died when Julia was twenty. She loved her father and was very sad to lose him, but he had limited her opportunities to meet people, especially a potential partner.

She and her sisters went to live with their older brother, Sam, whom she adored. Sam had recently married Emily Astor, who was from one of New York's wealthiest and most influential families. The young couple entertained and went out often. Julia now had the opportunity for a social life. She was very popular and attracted the interest of many young men. Soon she met her husband to be, Samuel Gridley Howe. He was twice her age but dashing, adventurous, and committed to many social reforms and causes in which she also believed. He was attracted to Julia because of her cleverness, her intelligence, and her many academic interests and ideas. Sam Howe had just returned from fighting in the Greek War of Independence and had written a book about his time as a soldier.

After they married, they moved into a wing of the Perkins Institute for the Blind in Boston, Massachusetts. Here, Sam Howe would be the director. The institute was not the cheeriest location for a young family. Like Julia's father, Sam was also strongly religious, but his religious beliefs were linked with his reformist views. He was an abolitionist and believed it was a religious duty to help those in need, such as people with disabilities, people in prison, or those with mental illness.

Reformer Dorothea Dix advocated for the establishment of facilities to house and treat the mentally ill. Sam Howe was one of her supporters.

MARRIED LIFE

Like her husband, Howe thought religion was not so much about what you believed but how you behaved to your fellow humans. She admired and agreed with her husband's work and beliefs. But trouble was coming for the couple because Sam did not want his wife to have a life outside the home. He believed a wife should support her husband in his beliefs and causes but should never speak publicly about those causes or involve herself in any outside activity that supported those causes.

Sam worked with Dorothea Dix, who was a reformer who advocated for better care for the mentally ill and improved conditions in the institutions where they lived. Dix was a lecturer, lobbyist, and advocate whom he admired for her many good works. This seems contradictory to his attitudes toward his wife's interests. Sam may have believed that a single woman (which Dix was) could behave differently than a married woman, which was common at the time.

Julia loved and respected her husband, so she accepted and followed his beliefs. They had six children together. She occupied herself with her role of wife and mother, as well as continuing her extensive reading and writing.

Both Julia and Sam attended a church whose minister, Theodore Parker, was an abolitionist and believed in women's rights. It was said that he kept a handgun on his desk, ready to defend the lives of the runaway slaves who were sheltering in his house on their way to freedom in Canada[1]. Julia developed a friendship with Parker, which brought intellectual stimulation and an outside perspective into her life.

But Howe was not a woman who could be submissive and live in isolation. She was restless and became impatient with the limitations of her life. She was trapped in a marriage that she found stifling, and she well understood how women, no matter how privileged, were powerless to control their own lives. Well educated and well read, she attended lectures and learned several languages. She was able to read classical Greek and explored classical literature in the original language of the writer. This was considered very unusual for a woman.

The marriage continued to deteriorate. Sam Howe controlled all the money Julia had inherited from her father. Because of the laws of the time, she had no legal standing to challenge how he managed this money. Poor investments diminished the wealth. Her husband clearly resented her desire for an independent life. The marriage was not improving. Divorce would have been a public scandal—and Julia would have lost the opportunity to be with her children. So she stayed and continued to educate herself and her children. She did travel to Europe with two of her children, which provided her with a much-needed separation from Sam.

Travel for an unescorted woman was daring and regarded by many as bold and unfeminine. For Howe, travel allowed her an opportunity to make decisions, to solve problems, and to plan for herself what she wanted to do and with whom. She traveled with friends who gave her the freedom and independence she craved. She talked directly with the men and women in the countries she visited. She learned their customs and beliefs. As time passed, Howe continued to write, publish her poetry, and become more involved in public life, despite her husband's wishes. Her poetry and plays contained references to her experience of being oppressed and controlled in her marriage, which infuriated her husband. But she kept writing and expressed through literature what she and many women experienced in their marriages and lives. It was rare for a woman to make public the unhappiness and oppression she was experiencing at home. Howe was a literary pioneer. Using her writing —even her fiction writing—she was able to open up discussion of generally taboo subjects such as domestic violence, infidelity, depression, suicide, gender identity, and other topics that confronted many women. Howe's marriage was stormy almost from the beginning, and she was known to have bouts of depression herself.

Her experience as a married woman was not uncommon in that time. A husband controlled every aspect of his wife's life. As with Howe, she had no options to stop her husband's decisions about using her money, controlling what happened to her children, or how she lived her life and what interests she could or could not pursue. Howe truly understood the vulnerable position of women in society. Even though she had social connections and some wealth, she did not have freedom. In her youth, she was controlled by her father until his death. Then in her marriage, her husband did not allow her to have a social life or to attend any events other than family or church gatherings on her own.

An amputation is performed in front of a hospital tent during the Civil War. The Howes advocated for improved health services for Union soldiers.

WAR WORK

Meanwhile, Howe's husband, Sam, continued his commitment to abolition work. She assisted him by helping him edit his abolition newspaper, the *Commentator*. The Fugitive Slave Act of 1850 infuriated many abolitionists because despite their beliefs, they were required by this law to return runaway slaves to their masters. This act only increased the sympathy of Northerners for the condition of those who were enslaved.

In 1856, Sam Howe led a group of antislavery settlers into Kansas to help tip the balance of voters so that Kansas would become a free state. There was so much violence in the state between pro- and antislavery advocates that the state became known as "Bloody Kansas." It was rumored that Sam Howe and several other men, including Julia's minister, Theodore Parker, had provided funds to John Brown, the radical abolitionist who attacked Harpers Ferry in hopes of obtaining weapons that would spark a slave rebellion. The attack failed, but Sam Howe, perhaps fearing the consequences of being a financial supporter of the attack, fled to Canada.

With the outbreak of the Civil War, both Julia and Sam became involved in health and hygiene reform on the battlefield. Despite their marital dif-ferences, they still had common interests in reform issues such as abolition and prison and asylum reform. Both were very concerned about the conditions experienced by Union soldiers when they were wounded or in the chaos of war. When the war first began, there were no ambulance services, no established hospitals near areas of conflict, no nursing services, and no way to identify the dead for burial. Many lives were lost from sickness and lack of medical care. To address this, the US government established the US Sanitary Commission in 1861 to care for sick and wounded Union soldiers and to assist them after they left military service. The South did not have such a commission and lost many soldiers because of the lack of medical care.

"THE BATTLE HYMN OF THE REPUBLIC"

Because of their support and volunteer work with the Sanitary Commission, the Howes were invited to Washington, DC, to meet President Lincoln. During their visit, they had an opportunity to visit the Union army, which was camped by the Potomac River. While they were there, they heard the troops singing a familiar song, a song that had different lyrics depending on whether the singer was a Northerner or a Southerner. A friend of Howe suggested that she write a new song for the Union troops to sing. The next morning, she got up, went to her desk, and wrote "The Battle Hymn of the Republic." It was an immediate success, not only

Among her other talents, Julia Ward Howe wrote the patriotic song "The Battle Hymn of the Republic." Howe's lyrics were first published in the *Atlantic Monthly* in 1862, and the song continues to be played at official government ceremonies and political gatherings today.

with the soldiers, but with the public as well. Howe had written poetry, biography, and plays, but her real fame came with writing this song. It reflected her religious nature and her passionate concern for peace and justice. She was a celebrity.

At this point in their lives, Sam stopped trying to limit her public appearances and her writing. She was famous in her own right—more well known by the public than he was. While he did not encourage or endorse her work, he gradually ceased to try to keep her in the home. He died in 1876, and after his death she turned her attention to many reform interests.

Howe had seen the terrible destruction caused by the Civil War—not only the suffering on the battlefield, but the damage done to families. The number of widows and orphaned children became a great concern for her. She worked to establish organizations that would care for the veterans and for the widows and children left by the war on both sides. Howe also worked to restore friendship among neighbors who had been divided by the war.

CLUBS

After the war, Howe became active in suffrage issues in the late 1860s. Because of her social standing, she was able to introduce the suffrage issue to influential and socially powerful women and gain their support. In 1869, Howe and Lucy

Stone became leaders of the American Woman Suffrage Association. Howe was president of the New England Suffrage Association and the Massachusetts Woman Suffrage Association, a new organization intended to build prosuffrage activity state by state. Howe enjoyed her participation in the New England Woman's Club. She called it "my dear Club!"[2] and acted as its president for almost forty years.

With the many organizations for women that exist today, it is hard to realize how important women's clubs were for women at the end of the nineteenth century. These clubs provided an environment where women could talk with each other about important social issues and not be silenced or disrespected by their husbands or fathers. The clubs provided a place where women could plan together and be respected and supported by each other. While Howe sometimes worried that clubs dismissed religion too much, the clubs offered a setting that was not dominated by clergy or other male religious leaders. The women were free to determine their own projects and set their own agendas.

Club women were not poor or uneducated, and they had powerful social connections, often through the men in their families. Since women did not control wealth, they had to influence wealth. No one was better connected or a better influencer than Julia Ward Howe. As one prominent Bostonian said, "When I want any-thing in Boston remedied, I go down to the New England Woman's Club!"

Another advantage for women's clubs was that they could be duplicated in different states and then coordinated by a federation of women's clubs in order to create a powerful, national lobby. Howe immediately saw the effectiveness of this kind of organization in helping petitioning drives and suffrage organizing by state. In 1892, she became president of the General Federation of Women's Clubs.

RELIGION AND PACIFISM

Howe never lost her strong belief in religion. She had been taught by her conservative father that there was only one set of correct religious beliefs and that everything else was wrong. However, her extensive reading, her travels, and her life experi-ences convinced her that there were other belief systems with which she agreed. She believed that religion must never demean any human being, be that person a woman, a person of color, or a person with a disability or a mental illness. The purpose of religion was to make each individual everything he or she can be. Howe often preached in both the Unitarian and Universalist churches. She convened a group of female ministers and also helped with the founding of the Free Religious Association.

This was a group that did not promote organized religion, but rather tried to promote religious activity that would help the progress of all people regardless of race or gender.

After seeing the horrors of the Civil War and learning of the devastation caused by the Franco-Prussian War in Europe, Howe came to believe that only a worldwide commitment to peace could stop war. She thought that women would be the most logical group to carry out this idea. She attempted to convene a world congress of women to work for peace. Howe also attempted to create a Mother's Day for Peace, a day that would both honor mothers and encourage world peace. She was not able to create this day, but later others were able to implement the Mother's Day holiday in the United States.

THE WOMEN'S CAUSE

After so many years of being controlled by her husband, Howe was free to engage in a reform very close to her heart: women's suffrage. She often said that in addition to the rewarding nature of the work, the company was delightful. She was particularly fond of Lucy Stone and worked closely with her on many projects. When she met Stone, Howe said, "Here stood the true woman, pure, noble, great-hearted, with the light of her good life shining in every feature of her face."[3]

Howe was in her early fifties before she had begun her work on woman's suffrage. She said, "Oh, had I earlier known the power, the nobility, the intelligence which lie within the range of true woman, I had surely lived more wisely and to better purpose."[4] Howe had originally scoffed at women's suffrage and the people who advocated for it. But in 1868, when she was asked if a meeting on suffrage could be convened in her name, she agreed. As her friend Tom Appleton said of her to her daughters, "Your mother's great importance to this cause is that she forms a bridge between the world of society and the world of reform."[5]

DISAGREEMENT IN THE WOMEN'S MOVEMENT

Both Julia Ward Howe and Lucy Stone agreed on both the principles and the strategies to move women's suffrage forward. But others did not. There had been violent disagreement between suffragists regarding what they should do about supporting or not supporting the Fourteenth and Fifteenth Amendments to the constitution. These amendments were originally designed to give equal rights to former slaves. Suffragists saw an opportunity to include women's rights in these amendments, too. But this did not happen. When it was clear that women's rights would not be included in the amendments, Susan B. Anthony and Elizabeth Cady Stanton blamed Lucy Stone,

Julia Ward Howe, and others for not standing firm on women's rights in the amendments.

On the other hand, black abolitionist Frederick Douglass accused Anthony of being racist and willing to deny black men the vote in the hopes that women could get the vote first. The Anthony faction created a new organization called the National Woman Suffrage Association (NWSA)

FREDERICK DOUGLASS (CIRCA 1818–1895)

Born into slavery, Douglass became a brilliant orator and a leader in the abolitionist movement. He wrote two autobiographies and was publisher of the *North Star,* **an abolitionist paper inspired by abolitionist William Lloyd Garrison's paper** *The Liberator.* **After fleeing from slavery, friends helped him to escape to England and purchase his freedom. Douglass returned to the United States, feeling strongly that his mission was there. In addition to his writing, publishing, and advocacy for abolition, Douglass worked for women's suffrage and other reforms. He believed that not making use of the intellect and talents of women resulted in a loss of half of the contributions that could be made to humanity. He believed in freedom for all peoples in America—black, white, Native American, male, and female.**

and the Stone/Howe faction created a new organization called the American Woman Suffrage Association (AWSA).

There were significant differences between the two organizations. The AWSA continued to include racial justice as one of its goals. It included men as full members of the organization. It was considered the more conservative organization and focused its work on the suffrage issue only, not on other women's issues. It was also against using militant or violent confrontations as a strategy. The AWSA's focus was on winning women's suffrage state by state, rather than working for a national constitutional amendment. The NWSA took the opposite point of view on all these issues. It was more militant, excluded males, wanted to work for a constitutional amendment to secure suffrage, wanted women's suffrage before black suffrage, and was interested in other women's rights issues such as making divorce laws easier and improving women's rights to own property.

Unfortunately, the two organizations remained separate until 1890. Both organizations published their own newspapers, and Julia Ward Howe was a major contributor to the AWSA's *Woman's Journal* for many years. Howe also became president of the Association for the Advancement of Women in 1881. It was an organization whose goals aligned with hers—promoting women's education and their involvement in service to the community.

Howe's AWSA and Anthony's NWSA organizations merged in 1890 to become the National American Woman Suffrage Association (NAWSA). This photograph shows NAWSA leaders after meeting with President Woodrow Wilson in 1917.

LATER YEARS AND HONORS

Julia Ward Howe made many contributions to the women's suffrage movement and to the betterment of the lives of Americans, both men and women. She was certainly most remembered for writing "The Battle Hymn of the Republic." Her accomplishments were in line with who she was as a person. Her own life experiences motivated her to work for the liberation and advancement of women. These things were not just concepts to Howe—they were struggles she had lived in her own life.

In addition to her many books, poems, articles, editorials, and leadership of many organizations promoting women's suffrage and other reformist causes, Howe was the first woman to be elected to the American Academy of Arts and Letters. This organization honored the very best in American literature, art, and music.

Howe died in Portsmouth, Rhode Island, at her own home. She was ninety-one. She had started life as a privileged young woman, but due to circumstances and her own talents, she became a working woman, making her living from her writing and lecturing. She was remembered by a large crowd of people who sang "The Battle Hymn of the Republic" at her memorial service. Two of her daughters wrote a biography of her life. She was honored by the US Postal Service by being represented on one of the stamps in the Great Americans series. Schools and neighborhoods were named after her, and her home in Rhode Island was included in the National Register of Historic Places.

Julia Ward Howe was a woman of many talents. She was a writer, a playwright, a poet, a reformer, a lyricist, an activist, an organizational leader, a socialite, a preacher, a lecturer, an abolitionist, and a suffragist. In one lifetime, she contributed many gifts to her fellow human beings, and perhaps none was more valuable than her dedication to the cause of women's rights.

CHAPTER THREE

LUCRETIA COFFIN MOTT

Lucretia Coffin was born in 1793 on the island of Nantucket, off the tip of Cape Cod in the state of Massachusetts. Her father, Thomas Coffin Jr., was a ship captain and made his living in the whaling trade. In the nineteenth century, whale blubber was used to make an oil that would fuel lamps and would be used in soapmaking, so it was an important industry.

Thomas Coffin would be away for long periods of time because a whale-hunting voyage could take a year or more. So Lucretia's mother, Anna Folger Coffin, started her own business. She became a shop owner. When weather was severe—which it often was in the winter—it was important that the island be supplied with basic food and other necessities. Anna saw an opportunity to meet this need, and she was very successful. Lucretia loved and admired her mother, who was an early role model

As a Quaker, Lucretia Coffin Mott rallied against the evils of slavery. Her experience being excluded from participating in various antislavery efforts compelled her to become involved in the women's rights movement.

Lucretia Mott.

for her. Anna and Thomas had five daughters and one son. Lucretia was the second-oldest child and always helped her mother with housework and with the other children. There was an older sister who may have had a disability and therefore was not able to help her mother as much.

Lucretia was always a small, slender person, but one who really enjoyed the food and the life on Nantucket. Her mother taught her to cook the delicious foods available on the island, and she always enjoyed preparing and eating food for the rest of her life.[1]

The Coffins were a Quaker family, and so boys and girls were considered equals, and both were worthy of an education. Lucretia began going to a Quaker school when she was four. When she was very young, she read a book on slavery written by an English Quaker woman named Priscilla Wakefield. The book described the many horrors of the Middle Passage (the sea voyage between Africa and the West Indies that captured slaves endured) as well as the other miseries of slave life in America.

There was no slavery in Nantucket, although many New Englanders profited from what was called the Triangular Trade. This was a three-sided route of sea trading in which slaves were bought on the west coast of Africa with rum that was made in New England, and then the slaves were brought to the West Indies and traded for sugar or molasses from which the New England rum was made.

Lucretia was shocked by what she read in Wakefield's book, and her conscience was troubled by what she had learned.

SCHOOL IN NEW YORK

Lucretia's father retired from whaling to become a merchant and moved the family to Boston. At the age of thirteen, Lucretia and her sister went to a residential school in New York named Nine Partners to continue their schooling. Lucretia soon became a "Hicksite,"[2] a committed Quaker abolitionist.

The superintendent of her school, James Mott Sr. (the grandfather of Lucretia's soon-to-be husband, James Mott Jr.), was a strong abolitionist and believed that Quakers had a responsibility to do more than just not be slaveholders themselves. He believed they should join in the fight to stop slavery everywhere. Mott boycotted (refused to buy for ethical or political reasons) any goods that were related to slavery, such as any cotton cloth or clothing or cane sugar.

Lucretia became friends with James Mott's granddaughter and got to know her brother James Mott Jr., too. Both James Mott Jr. and Lucretia became teachers at the Nine Partners School. Once again, Lucretia was to see and experience an injustice. James made more than twice the salary she did as a teacher! She did not blame James personally but began to see that, despite her Quaker upbringing based on gender equality, the rest of the world was not that way.

Lucretia's family had since moved to Philadelphia, and her father had sold everything he had to start a new manufacturing business. Lucretia rejoined her family and introduced James to them. James became a boarder (a person who pays rent for a place to stay and for food). He soon became Lucretia's father's business partner.

From a Photograph by F. Gutekunst in 1863.

MARRIAGE, MONEY, LOSS, AND FAITH

James Mott and Lucretia Coffin married in 1811. Just a few years later, Lucretia's father died, and the family inherited significant debt from his

Lucretia Coffin married James Mott in 1811, and the couple raised a family that was active in social reform.

business. His widow, Anna, once again set herself up in a shop and began to pay down the debt.

Lucretia's husband's family was also experiencing financial problems. Since her father's business had failed, her husband, James, had to find new work. He went into business with his uncle. He also did not want to trade in any goods that were products of slave labor. So while his uncle dealt in cotton cloth, James moved toward selling wool cloth.

Lucretia and James Mott had six children, five of whom survived into adulthood. Their first son died when he was three years old. Lucretia was devastated. The tragedy also made her think deeply about her religion and what it meant to her. She began to think of God as an inner presence that was with her always. She began to speak of this as an inner light that was a source of understanding for her.

About a year after the death of her son, Mott "spoke" during a meeting of the Friends (Quakers). The Quaker form of worship was to sit quietly together until someone was moved to speak. Mott was afraid but wanted to share what she was experiencing with others. Her words were admired by the Quakers, and she spoke again during other meetings. She gained confidence in herself, and in 1821, she was recognized as a minister.

James was always supportive of Lucretia and shared her antislavery beliefs. Ever since her childhood, Mott was strong in her beliefs and opinions. She never feared or avoided conflict, and she had a talent for bringing people together to resolve disagreement.

And there was plenty of that, even among the usually peaceful Quakers. There was a custom among Quakers that if a member did not live according to Quaker rules, that person could be disowned by the group and none of Quaker society would have anything to do with him or her. This had happened to several of Mott's friends who had gone with their children to hear a progressive Quaker speaker. They were disowned as Quakers. This greatly angered Mott. But more was to come. The same was to happen to her family. Her sister Martha was disowned for marrying "out of meeting" (not marrying a Quaker).

Adding to her internal conflicts was her increasing need to act against slavery. Both in her home and in her Quaker community, there were challenges. At home, the Motts' prosperity included some dealing in cotton cloth and sugar. Mott determined that their household would have to boycott those products, so she went without her beloved ice cream and the children went without candy. James was pleasantly surprised that he prospered in the wool business.

THE BUSINESS OF ABOLITION AND WOMEN'S RIGHTS

In the Quaker community, conflict continued between the Hicksite faction and the rest of the Quakers. Mott was a fiery speaker and encouraged all Quakers to join the boycott against slave products. Soon Mott gained recognition for her

WILLIAM LLOYD GARRISON (1805–1879)

William Lloyd Garrison was a leader in the American abolition and suffrage movements. He was the cofounder and editor of *The Liberator,* which he published until after the Civil War. The paper advocated for the emancipation of all slaves immediately. Others favored gradual emancipation. Garrison was perhaps the most well-known of all abolitionists. He was a passionate and articulate spokesman for the cause of abolition, and he was an early believer in nonviolence and passive resistance. He was a founder of the American Anti-Slavery Society and recruited many famous abolitionist lecturers, including Angelina Grimké, Lucy Stone, and Abby Kelley. He was also a strong advocate for the cause of women's suffrage.

William Lloyd Garrison's newspaper, the *Liberator*, was an influential voice in the abolitionist movement in the decades leading up to the Civil War. Like many abolitionists, Garrison also took up the cause of women's rights.

speaking skills as an abolitionist and was traveling all over the New England area. Mott developed a very close and inspiring friendship with William Lloyd Garrison, the famous abolitionist.

But Mott was faced with a dilemma. Although she was sought after for her abolition speaking, she and other women abolitionists were not allowed to be a part of most organized abolitionist groups. So in 1833, Mott helped found the Philadelphia Female Anti-Slavery Society.

She also helped to organize the First Anti-Slavery Convention of American Women in 1837. Along with antislavery orators such as Angelina Grimké, Mott was sharply criticized for speaking to mixed audiences of men and women. She, like the Grimké sisters, was now speaking for both abolition and women's rights.

The Mott household was often full of guests— black, white, male, and female—who shared lively conversation on many reform topics. The fact that Mott entertained African Americans, and included them in her organizations, angered many proslavery factions in the Philadelphia area. Like other abolitionists and women's rights advocates, Mott was often faced with hostile mobs. For the poor, or those who were barely getting by, the possibility of the labor market being flooded with freed slaves was a frightening thought. This fear generated great anger at the abolitionists, who were working to end slavery.

The Motts and other abolitionists and antislavery advocates had raised funds to build a venue to be the location for abolitionist speaking activity. Many who had meeting halls large enough to host the crowds that would come to hear people like Angela Grimké and Lucretia Mott were too frightened of the hostility against abolitionists and so would not open their buildings to them.

So when the 1838 Anti-Slavery Convention was held in Pennsylvania Hall in Philadelphia, many abolitionists were delighted to have a beautiful, large meeting place where they could speak to the public about their cause. But trouble was brewing. A huge crowd had gathered, angered as they saw black women going in and out of the hall. On the evening of May 16, the mayor himself came to talk to the crowd and told them the convention had been cancelled, hoping that this would break up the crowd. He then went to Mott and the other white convention leaders, asking them to not let any of the black females attend the convention. Mott disagreed with this. Instead, she instructed all the women to leave the hall together, with each white woman walking with a black woman.

After the women had left Pennsylvania Hall, the mayor locked the doors and left without posting any guards. The mob had increased to seventeen thousand people, and it was looking to cause some destruction.[3] They broke into Pennsylvania Hall and looted what they could and set fire to the rest.

By dawn, the building was in ruins. And the danger was not over.

Lucretia and James Mott walked with a large group of friends and convention attendees to their home, to wait quietly for further news of the mob. Mott's son heard the mob coming and called out to his family. But amazingly, the mob passed by the Mott home! A friend of the Motts had directed the mob to another area and away from the Motts. They were safe—for the moment. But the division within the Anti-Slavery Society remained divided over the role of women and the rights they should or should not have.

TRAVELS ACROSS THE SEA

Mott had a history of severe digestive problems, and after the violence at the Anti-Slavery Convention of American Women and the continuing disagreement within the Anti-Slavery Society she was not feeling well. In the spring of 1840, both the Motts were elected as delegates to the World's Anti-Slavery Convention to be held in London, England, in June. Being always homesick for her beloved Nantucket, Mott was excited about the sea voyage, as well as the London conference.

But the issue of women's rights seemed to follow Mott across the Atlantic. When the Motts arrived at the convention, they were dismayed to hear that 90 percent of the all-male convention

WHAT WAS THE UNDERGROUND RAILROAD?

The Underground Railroad was a secret network of routes and safe places to stay for escaped slaves. The slaves were helped along the way by people who were sympathetic to their suffering. Most were abolitionists or people who wanted to help them to a new life of freedom in the northern states or Canada. The escaped slaves usually traveled by night to avoid being seen by bounty hunters (people who were paid by slave masters and others to recapture their slaves) or by citizens who just wanted to make money by returning a slave to his or her master. The Underground Railroad followed secret routes to the North, often following the North Star to stay on the right track. It also used railroad terminology as a sort of code to keep the work secret. "Stations" were safe places to stay for runaway slaves; "conductors" helped to lead the slaves to the North; "agents" were people who helped the slaves get in contact with the Underground Railroad; "station masters" invited fugitive slaves into their homes; "passengers" were the escaping slaves who "rode" the railroad.

THE EMANCIPATOR—EXTRA. February 24th, 1838.

ANTI-SLAVERY CONVENTION.

The undersigned invite all the citizens of Connecticut friendly to the immediate emancipation of the slaves of our country, to send delegates to a Convention to be held at Hartford, on Wednesday, the 28th of February, 1838, in order to form a STATE ANTI-SLAVERY SOCIETY. Individuals in this State, and from other States, holding the principles of Anti-Slavery Societies, are also invited to attend the Convention.

We propose the formation of a State Society, that our influence may be more efficient, and that the great cause in which we are engaged, may be carried on with more energy.

We believe we have a *right*, and that it is our *duty*, to do all that we can, consistently with the Constitution and Laws, to abolish slavery in our land : we entertain no Utopian project of "letting loose" all the slaves : but we propose to have them placed under equal and just laws ; to deliver them from the yoke of oppression, and give them liberty.

We believe the system of slavery in our country *ought* to be abolished, because it is fraught with evil to the slave and the slave holder ; and we believe it *can* be done, because it has been done in other countries, not only without injury, but with positive good to all parties. We believe it *ought* to be done because it is *wrong* in itself ; contrary to human rights ; and contrary to the spirit of the Bible.

We believe that a state of things which forbids the reading of the Bible ; which deprives men of property in themselves ; which does not recognize the institution of marriage ; which is continually rending asunder the most tender ties ; and the habitual tendency of which is to degrade men to the condition of brutes, *ought* to be changed immediately.

We know that we have no power, and no right to abrogate the laws of the slave-holding States ; and we disclaim it. We do not propose to the slave, to arise, and vindicate his rights ; but we propose the only course which will prevent it.

The only means we wish to use are a *moral influence* ; a concentration of public opinion ; a diffusion of light and knowledge on the subject ; which will convince and persuade our southern brethren that it is not only *right* for them to free the slaves, but that the best interests of our country *require* it.

[Numerous columns of signatories' names follow, arranged by county; individual names are not legibly reproducible.]

This broadside invited citizens of Connecticut to attend an anti-slavery convention to be held on February 24, 1838. Such conventions were held in many US states and abroad, such as the World's Anti-Slavery Convention in London, where Mott met Elizabeth Cady Stanton.

had voted to exclude women as delegates to the convention.[4] So Mott could attend only as a visitor. But despite the rejection of women delegates, Mott found an opportunity to tour and speak to various groups in London about abolition and women's rights. She was an admired and influential visitor. While she could not be seated as a delegate, she was often engaged in arguing with British abolitionists who did not support women's rights.

It was at the London convention that Mott met fellow abolitionist and women's rights advocate Elizabeth Cady Stanton, whose husband was also a delegate at the World's Anti-Slavery Convention. The two women became friends and decided that when they returned to the United States, they would plan a women's rights convention.

ON THE ROAD AGAIN

When Mott returned to America, she felt the need to go on a speaking tour to continue to advocate for abolition. Her travels took her into areas of the South, where she had a chance to talk face-to-face with slave owners. Amazingly, many times these men acknowledged that in their heart of hearts, they knew slavery was wrong.

In her southern travels, Mott met the then president of the United States, John Tyler, who was much impressed with her eloquence and perseverance. He said that when the meeting was over,

"I would like to hand Mr. Calhoun over to you."
Congressman John C. Calhoun was a famous
debater and leader of the South.[5]

Mott continued to meet resistance from the
more conservative Quakers. As a minister, she had
been disciplined and silenced, but not disowned by
the Quaker leadership. But this treatment hurt and
angered her because she believed so strongly that
Quakers had a responsibility to lead on matters of
abolition and women's rights.

ANOTHER LOSS

As strong willed and feisty as Lucretia Mott was,
she continued to look up to and rely on her mother
for approval and encouragement. Ever since her
childhood on Nantucket, Anna Coffin had been a
role model as well as a mother to her. Her mother
lived with Mott in Philadelphia and was a constant
source of support for her.

But in 1844, both Mott and her mother came
down with a serious respiratory illness. Both
women were fighting for their lives. When Mott
became aware of how ill her mother was, she
demanded to be wrapped in blankets and brought
to her mother's bedside. Anna died on March 26,
and Mott was crushed by her loss.

Though she deeply mourned her mother's death,
she rallied and regained her strength and began
to fulfill her role as matriarch (female head) of the

family. She found renewal in household tasks and family matters. Mott was seldom without knitting or sewing in her hands, and she was always ready to help bake or cook for weddings or other family events.

There were also opportunities for her to help the poor in Philadelphia. Many of these men and women were hand weavers who were being replaced by more mechanized processes for making cloth. Mott was appalled at the manufacturers who were seemingly unaffected by the suffering this had caused. Workers went on strike to fight for a living wage. The workers' families were hungry and sick. Mott showed not only her compassion, but her extraordinary organizational skills to bring assistance and comfort to these families. But she knew that it was very little help and did not get to the root of the problem. The workers went hungry, and the factory owners did not give them a decent wage. "With the oppressor there is power," she said.[6]

SENECA FALLS

The plans for a women's rights convention discussed in London by Mott and Elizabeth Cady Stanton took some years to materialize. Stanton was living in Boston and enjoying an active and intellectually stimulating life, as well as raising a large family of young children. Mott visited often, and they continued to discuss the convention. Mott was fully involved in speaking for abolition and reform issues and trying to maintain herself in a conservative Quaker society.

The Motts were in New York State visiting friends and also visiting a small Seneca reservation that the Quakers were supporting. The Motts were joined in the nearby town of Waterloo by Stanton. She had purchased a house in a small, rural town in upstate New York called Seneca Falls. She was eager for educated, adult company and was delighted when she was invited to join the Motts.

A small group of women, including Mott and Stanton, sat together around a small tea table and decided to host a women's convention in Seneca Falls. After they had announced the event, they became energized with planning and organizing the event. Together, they came up with the idea of modifying the Declaration of Independence into a document that would speak to the importance of freedom for women. They created the Declaration of Sentiments that begins, "We hold these truths to be self-evident: that all men *and women* are created equal . . ."

Initially, only women were to be invited. As the day of the convention approached, everyone was worried that no one would come. As James Mott was driving his wife into Seneca Falls, they were overwhelmed at the number of coaches and people clogging the streets. The convention had

THE FIRST CONVENTION

EVER CALLED TO DISCUSS THE

Civil and Political Rights of Women,

SENECA FALLS, N. Y., JULY 19, 20, 1848.

WOMAN'S RIGHTS CONVENTION.

A Convention to discuss the social, civil, and religious condition and rights of woman will be held in the Wesleyan Chapel, at Seneca Falls, N. Y., on Wednesday and Thursday, the 19th and 20th of July current; commencing at 10 o'clock A. M. During the first day the meeting will be exclusively for women, who are earnestly invited to attend. The public generally are invited to be present on the second day, when Lucretia Mott, of Philadelphia, and other ladies and gentlemen, will address the Convention.*

Mott, Stanton, and others organized the historic Woman's Rights Convention at Seneca Falls, New York, in 1848. At the convention, Mott was free to exhibit her dazzling oratorial skills as the featured speaker.

been successful in attracting both women and men. When they entered the meeting place, Mott and the other women decided to ask James Mott to chair the convention and to manage the order of the speakers.

One of the resolutions to be adopted addressed suffrage for women. When Stanton made Mott aware of the resolution, Mott was very surprised. Up to this point, Mott had not given much consideration to voting and the elective process. Because she had been supporting William Lloyd Garrison in his resistance to government dominating individuals through destructive institutions such as slavery, she had not given much value to having the vote. But in discussions with Stanton, Anthony, and others, she quickly saw that if men had the vote, women should have it, too. Others attending the convention were also in doubt about the suffrage resolution. One of the attendees spoke powerfully for women's suffrage. Frederick Douglass's eloquence helped the suffrage resolution to pass.

Following the convention, Mott continued to devote herself to both abolition and women's rights. In 1850, she wrote her "Discourse on Women," setting forth her philosophy on the rights of women. As a pacifist, the Civil War caused her great sadness. Yet at the end of the war, the slaves were free, a goal she had worked for with great dedication. In 1868, she chaired the annual meeting of the American Equal Rights Association, which dissolved over a disagreement about whether the Fourteenth Amendment should include women as well as freed slaves. Mott joined with Anthony and Stanton to form the National Woman Suffrage Association (NWSA). This organization was in competition with the American Woman Suffrage Association (AWSA), led by suffragists Lucy Stone and Julia Ward Howe. The NWSA believed that suffrage should come through a federal amendment to the constitution, which was how women did actually get the right to vote.

Mott continued to travel and speak, though she had grown frailer. She served as vice president of the Universal Peace Union and the Pennsylvania Peace Society. She and her husband had been active in the creation of a Quaker college, Swarthmore, which they both insisted be a co-educational institution.

HONORS AND REMEMBRANCES

Lucretia Coffin Mott delivered her last public speech at the thirtieth anniversary celebration of the Seneca Fall Convention in Rochester, NY. She died at her at her home in Chelton Hills, outside of Philadelphia, that same year, at the age of eighty-five. She was remembered as being one of the earliest—and most effective—leaders in the American suffrage movement. Unlike many people, she grew more radical as she aged. Her belief

The portrait monument to the pioneers of the women's suffrage movement features statues of Elizabeth Cady Stanton, Susan B. Anthony, and Lucretia Mott. The monument is located in the Capitol building rotunda in Washington, DC.

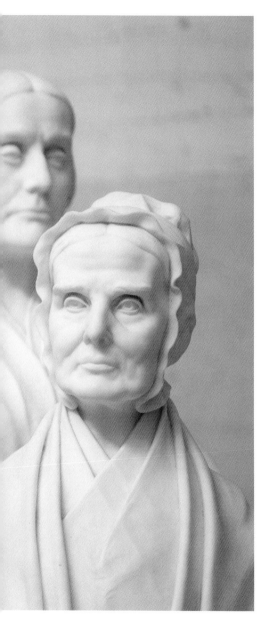

that working for reform was one of the most important ways to demonstrate religious faith increased as she worked for black and female suffrage, for temperance issues, and for peace. Like Matilda Joslyn Gage, Mott saw that not being able to vote was just one of many barriers against women.

Mott was a woman devoted to her family, who enjoyed the tasks of maintaining a home. But she worked unceasingly for laws that would expand women's rights, including equal property rights, an equal education, access to work in all the professions, including ministry, and the right to always have access to their children. Mott, Stanton, and Anthony were all included in a sculpture that is located in the US Capitol in Washington, DC. The monument honors all three respected leaders of the women's suffrage movement.

Mott is also celebrated through the Lucretia Mott Award, which is presented to an outstanding American woman whose achievements advance the goals of women and girls, and whose life work shows her commitment to equality. Previous award recipients include Martin Luther King Jr.'s widow, Coretta Scott King, and feminist activist Gloria Steinem.

Not only was Mott acclaimed as one of the greatest American women of her century, but she also continues to be an example and a guiding light to those advocates for human rights who continue her work.

CHAPTER FOUR

LUCY STONE

Lucy Stone was born in rural Massachusetts in 1818. Her father was originally a teacher when he was young but then returned to being a tanner, the trade his father had taught him. A tanner is a person who makes shoes, gloves, and other items from animal hides. Later, he became a farmer because his wife felt farm life would be a better environment for the children. She was a gentle person, and obedient to her husband, as the times demanded. Lucy's father was the ruler of their household. As she later said, "There was only one will in our home, and that was my father's."[1] Though constantly overworked, her mother was loyal and devoted to her husband and strongly believed it was his right to rule over the household as he did.

The night before Lucy came into the world, her mother milked eight cows because the men on the farm had to harvest the hay crop before it was

Lucy Stone is considered by many to be the heartbeat of the women's rights movement in the United States. Her speeches and writings on the plight of women influenced many, including fellow leaders Susan B. Anthony and Elizabeth Cady Stanton, to fight for women's suffrage.

spoiled by rain. Lucy was the eighth of nine children. When her mother was told that she had given
birth to a girl, she said "Oh, dear! I am sorry it is a
girl. A woman's life is so hard!"[2]

Lucy grew up loving nature and the beauty of
it. She would often go to a beautiful hilltop called
Coy's Hill near her home to watch the sunset with
her sisters. She was known as a fearless, truth-
ful, hardworking child, and she was very good at
school. Her reputation as being fearless would
continue throughout her life. While she was often
afraid for the safety of others, she never seemed to
fear for herself.

Even from a young age, she was very aware of
how hard her mother had to work, and she would
get up before dawn to get her chores done so she
could help her mother. In addition to farm chores,
Lucy was also expected to help her father make
shoes. She was faster than her brothers and sisters, and her father expected that she would make
more shoes than the other children. Lucy's first
experience with discrimination was in her home,
where her father gave preference to her brothers
for an education, even though they were not as
bright as she.

The family had only a few books, but they did
subscribe to several newspapers, including *The
Liberator*. This paper was dedicated to the abolition of slavery in America. It was published by one
of the greatest leaders of the abolition movement,

William Lloyd Garrison. He would play a very important role in Lucy Stone's life.

Lucy realized that if she wanted to go to college and pursue an education, she would have to do it on her own. She could expect no help from her father. Lucy began teaching in her mid-teens and supplemented her income by picking chestnuts and selling them to get money to buy her books for school.

EARLY INFLUENCES

Stone was determined to attend the recently established Mount Holyoke Seminary for girls. Founded by Mary Lyon, the seminary offered young women an education similar to what men would have received.

She had heard Mary Lyon speak when she was attending a sewing circle/fund-raiser for Lyon's school. At the time, Stone was sewing a shirt for a male seminary student. She realized that the male seminarian was making more by teaching for one week than Stone would make in a month. Disgusted, she stopped sewing the shirt and hoped that no one else would finish it either. This was the first of many experiences Stone had illustrated that women were consistently underpaid for the work they did compared to men.

Stone became a member of the Orthodox Congregational Church—also while she was in

MARY LYON: PIONEER FOR WOMEN'S EDUCATION (1797–1846)

Mary Lyon founded the first college for women in New England. She began teaching in her teens and taught at several schools before founding Mount Holyoke Seminary. Despite hard economic times and prejudice against educating women, Lyon was able to raise enough funds to open the seminary. She ran the school and also found time to teach chemistry to her students. Lyon required that her pupils take math and science courses. She also required that the young women who attended the school do chores and other housekeeping tasks in order to keep the tuition low enough so that all young woman with very little money could attend.[3]

her teens—and during a discussion on the issue of slavery, she raised her hand to cast her vote against slavery. She was told that her vote did not count, even though she was a member, because women could not vote. She was infuriated, and each time a vote was called, she raised her hand to vote. The issue of slavery was beginning to divide churches and their parishioners. Women such as Abby Kelley and the Grimké sisters, Angelina and Sarah, began to speak publicly against slavery. The division on the issue of slavery was emotionally

Mary Lyon was an early advocate for the education of women in the United States. Lyon founded the Wheaton Female Seminary and the Mount Holyoke Female Seminary, which Stone attended for a short time.

intense. When Angelina Grimké spoke in favor of abolition at the Boston State House, it was burned down the next day. Stone was moved and inspired by the work of these women, and she became a strong abolitionist herself.

EDUCATION AND ABOLITION

It took Stone nine years to save up enough money to attend Oberlin College. Women and people of color were accepted as students by the college, and many were very poor. Stone had hoped to start teaching in her first year but discovered that the teachers had a rule that prevented first-year students from teaching until they had proven themselves of good moral character and responsible in their work with the students. Stone wrote to her brother Bowman, who was a minister, asking him to speak on her behalf. He did, and Stone was allowed to teach in her first year of college. Like all the students, she was required to participate in household chores. Stone was known to prop her Greek textbook on a shelf and read it while she was drying dishes.

Stone also taught runaway slaves who had escaped from their owners and had settled near Oberlin College. Oberlin College was a stop on the Underground Railroad. Those who helped the escaped slaves were always in great danger because they had broken a law, the Fugitive Slave

Act. The Fugitive Slave Act was a law passed by the US Congress in 1850. It said that all escaped slaves should be captured and returned to their owners, even if the slaves had reached a free state (a free state was a state where slavery was illegal). This law was an attempt by slave-holding states to discourage slaves from trying to run away and to stop northern abolitionists and others from helping them find freedom when they did escape. This law outraged the abolitionists, who feared that it would greatly strengthen the institution of slavery.

While Oberlin College favored abolition, it did not support the radical "Garrisonian abolitionists," such as Stone. This group of abolitionists condemned proslavery churches and clergy and also supported women speaking publicly against slavery. Many in the group even withheld support for the US Constitution because it sanctioned slavery.

THE FIRST WOMAN GRADUATE

It was at Oberlin that Stone began to question why a woman should give up her name when she married, and she determined that she would always keep her own name. Not that getting married was something that Stone was interested in, considering her knowledge of the oppressive laws that women faced if they did marry. She had had offers of marriage and was considered attractive, even though her father said, "Lucy's face is

WHAT WERE BLOOMERS?

Bloomers were a new type of dress for women. They were named after a woman, Amelia Bloomer, who wore them and made them popular. Bloomers were an answer to the uncomfortable and confining clothes that women had to wear in the nineteenth century. They were also known as "the freedom dress" or "the hygiene dress." They consisted of a small jacket, a full skirt to just below the knees, and full-length pants underneath. Suffragists Susan B. Anthony, Elizabeth Cady Stanton, Sarah Grimké, and Lucy Stone wore them at times, but in Stone's case, it became a distraction to the larger message of women's rights she was trying to communicate.

like a blacksmith's apron; it keeps off the sparks."[4] Despite this cruel remark, Stone declared she would never marry and wished that she were even plainer looking so that she could discourage any man from proposing marriage. But even her father had to respect Stone's courage and determination. By her third year at Oberlin, her gruff father had to admit she had grit, and he told her that she would not have to work to keep herself in college. He would pay for all of her expenses.

Stone held the first National Woman's Rights Convention in 1850 at Brinley Hall in Worcester, Massachusetts. The meeting space was located on the top floor of this three-story structure.

Even though it was a progressive school, Oberlin followed conventional attitudes about women speaking in public. It did not allow female students to speak at graduation. Stone had grown very interested in public speaking and wanted to write and deliver a commencement address. Oberlin would not permit her to do this. They would permit her to write the address, but a man would have to deliver the speech. She declined this arrangement and graduated from the college in 1847. She was the first woman from her native state of Massachusetts to receive a college degree.

A NEW CAREER

It did not seem that there was much likelihood of Stone beginning a career in public speaking for the cause of abolition, since a career in public speaking—and most professional careers—were not open to women. But Stone was a determined woman. She made her first public speech on abolition at her brother Bowman's church. One year later, she had been hired by the abolitionist leader and publisher of *The Liberator*, William Lloyd Garrison, to lecture on behalf of the Anti-Slavery Society.

Stone had an extraordinary voice. Although she was a small, quiet woman, she was an outstanding orator. She had a voice that was described as "like a silver bell." She could project her voice to the back of the meeting hall.

She never lost her fearlessness, even though she was frequently threatened by mob violence. In one incident, she was accompanied by abolitionist Stephen Foster when an angry mob surrounded them. Stone called to Foster to get away before he was attacked, but he asked her who would then protect her from the mob. She quickly turned to a large man carrying a club who was approaching her and said, "This man will!" The man was so shocked and impressed, he offered to escort her to the site of her lecture.

SPEAKING FOR THE WOMEN

Stone began to weave the issues of women's rights into her abolition lectures. When the general agent of the Anti-Slavery Society pointed out to her what she was doing, she said to him, "Well, Mr. May, I was a woman before I was an abolitionist. I must speak for the women."[5]

She told the Anti-Slavery Society that she would retire as their lecturer. But Stone was one of their very best speakers, and they did not want to lose her. She agreed that she would continue to speak on behalf of abolition on the weekends and would speak for women's rights during the week. Stone began to speak for the women,and to accept a small fee from the contributions of the audience. She had no society or group supporting her, and no one paying her for her work. She was on her own. And she succeeded, becoming one of the most well-paid lecturers for the cause of women's rights.

But there were still painful experiences that she had to endure. Stone often lectured about inaccurate translations of Greek and Latin classics that were included in the Bible. These misleading translations were the source of the belief that women should not speak publicly in church. Because she questioned these translations, she was accused of disagreeing with scriptures and was expelled from her Congregationalist church.

Interest in women's rights and women's suffrage was growing due in large part to the tireless speaking and advocacy of Stone. Stone led the way in convening the First National Women's Rights Convention in Worcester, Massachusetts, in 1850. Susan B. Anthony read the report of Stone's speech at this convention and said it motivated her to become involved with the fight for women's suffrage.

LOVE, MARRIAGE, AND FAMILY LIFE

Following the convention, Stone traveled all over the United States and Canada lecturing on suffrage and women's rights. She continued to attend the annual women's rights conventions and presided over the seventh one. During her travels, she met her future husband, Henry Blackwell, the brother of physicians Elizabeth and Emily Blackwell. He had helped Stone by organizing a lecture schedule for her in Ohio. He shared her strong convictions about abolition and women's rights. Blackwell rescued a young female slave who had been brought by train into Pennsylvania—a free state—by her master. Blackwell asked the girl if she wished to be free, and he helped her to escape after she said yes.

Although Stone had sworn she would never marry, her admiration and love for Blackwell grew as they got to know each other. He asked her to marry him, but she said she could not. She did not object to him but rather to the injustices she would be subjected to as a married woman. It took Blackwell two years to convince her that they could create a truly equal marriage in which both of them would have the same rights. Their 1855 marriage ceremony would not include any words suggesting that the wife would "obey" her husband. The ceremony also included a protest against marital laws that removed the freedom of women to control their own income and activities outside of the home. As she had decided while at Oberlin College, Stone kept her name and was addressed as "Mrs. Stone." The couple continued to work together to advocate for women's rights and suffrage.

The marriage occurred when Stone was thirty-seven. When she was thirty-nine, she had her only child, a daughter named Alice Stone Blackwell. Stone believed that a child should have both her parents' names. Unlike Stone's experience, Alice had the support of both her parents in pursuing an education and becoming involved in the suffrage and women's rights movements.

While Stone never stopped writing and advocating for women, she did feel that she could not travel and maintain a lecture schedule with a young child at home. Susan B. Anthony was angry at

Stone for spending her time keeping house and tending a baby. She felt the same about Elizabeth Cady Stanton and her seven children. Anthony never married.

However, during her time at home, Stone made a dramatic demonstration of her personal commitment to women's rights. The family home, a cottage in Orange, New Jersey, was in Stone's name. She refused to pay taxes on the house, protesting that there should be "no taxation without representation," and since women could not vote, she was not represented at any level of government. Her refusal to pay these taxes resulted in the sale of all the family's household goods, including baby Alice's cradle. Fortunately, a neighbor bought Stone's household possessions and returned them to her.

CONFLICT IN THE SUFFRAGE MOVEMENT

The period after the Civil War was known as Reconstruction. It was during this time that Congress tried to make sure that freed slaves actually had the rights of citizenship, including enfranchisement (the right to vote). There were three amendments passed to make sure freed slaves would have these rights. Two of them had great significance for leaders of the suffrage movement. The Fourteenth Amendment stated that former slaves were entitled to equal rights under the law. The Fifteenth Amendment gave former slaves the right to vote. Disagreement over the wording of these two amendments started an enormous conflict and created a huge split in the women's suffrage movement.

While living in New Jersey with her family, Stone became president of the New Jersey Woman Suffrage Association. She then worked to establish the New England Woman Suffrage Association, in which she would be active after the family moved to Boston in 1869. She also was a member of the executive committee of the American Equal Rights Association. This group grew out of the Eleventh National Woman's Rights Convention. Its purpose was to work for equal suffrage for both women and African Americans.

It was this group that created the anger and conflict between Stone and Susan B. Anthony and Elizabeth Cady Stanton, which would continue throughout their lives. And it would cause division among the suffrage movement.

The American Equal Rights Association's purpose was to coordinate the work for suffrage for both African Americans and women. The American Equal Rights Association supported the passage of the Fifteenth Amendment. Anthony and Stanton were against its passage because they believed that the amendment's reference to "male" would obtain voting rights for black men only.

Lucy Stone had gone to Washington, DC, to lobby for the cause of including women in the

Fifteenth Amendment. But she was not successful. Stone believed that it was better to assure the
vote for black men, and then to use this success
to strengthen the campaign for women's suffrage.
Support for the Fifteenth Amendment included
many women and most of the men in the organization. Stanton and especially Anthony fought bitterly
with those who supported this amendment, however, and they never forgave Stone's failure to join
them. Anthony and Stanton both believed women's
suffrage should have come ahead of black male
suffrage.

Following this battle, Anthony and Stanton
formed the National Woman Suffrage Association
(NWSA) in May 1869, leaving Stone, Julia Ward
Howe, and other suffragist leaders to create the
American Woman Suffrage Association (AWSA).
Howe, who brought considerable social prestige
and influence, was elected president. Stone raised
funds to start the AWSA's *Woman's Journal*, a
publication dedicated to educating women about
women's rights and suffrage. Stone became editor
of the publication, and it was more successful than
the NWSA's *Revolution in* presenting the women's
movement as a mainstream issue. Her first edi-
torial was "The Legal Rights of Mothers to Their
Children."

Stone continued to help the AWSA to organize petition drives for women's suffrage, arranged
legislative hearings, organized conventions, set up

Stone established the periodical *Woman's Journal* with her husband Henry in 1870 as an alternative to the *Revolution*. Their daughter Alice took over editing duties after Henry's death. *Woman's Journal* was published for more than sixty years.

meetings and prepared presentations to legislators, wrote press releases, carried out fund-raising, and wrote letters to supporters and legislators. She helped suffragists in many states to lobby for improved laws for women. Her eloquence helped to pass Canada's Woman's Property Law. She worked to include women's suffrage in both the Republican and Democratic parties' platforms (issues that each party supported) but was only able to achieve inclusion in the Prohibition and Labor party platforms. Along with suffrage leaders like Abby Kelley Foster, Stone continued to protest paying taxes without the right to vote.

Before she died, Stone saw the rift between the National Woman Suffrage Association and the American Woman Suffrage Association healed. Her daughter, Alice, and Stanton's daughter, Harriot Stanton Blatch, were both involved in bringing the two women together. Stone was the chair of the executive committee, and Elizabeth Cady Stanton served as president of the new organization, the National American Woman Suffrage Association (NAWSA). Both women wanted to see the old divisions come to an end.

RECOGNITION

Stone's last speech was given at the Columbian Exposition in 1893. Her friends, anxious to honor her, commissioned sculptor Ann Whitney to make a

The Revolution.

PRINCIPLE, NOT POLICY: JUSTICE, NOT FAVORS.

VOL. I.—NO. 1.   NEW YORK, WEDNESDAY, JANUARY 8, 1868. $2.00 A YEAR.

The Revolution;

THE ORGAN OF THE

NATIONAL PARTY OF NEW AMERICA.

PRINCIPLE, NOT POLICY—INDIVIDUAL RIGHTS AND RESPONSIBILITIES.

THE REVOLUTION WILL ADVOCATE:

1. In POLITICS—Educated Suffrage, Irrespective of Sex or Color; Equal Pay to Women for Equal Work; Eight Hours Labor; Abolition of Standing Armies and Part; Despotisms. Down with Politicians—Up with the People!

2. In RELIGION—Deeper Thought; Broader Idea; Science not Superstition; Personal Purity; Love to Man as well as God.

3. In SOCIAL LIFE—Morality and Reform; Practical Education, not Theoretical; Facts not Fiction; Virtue not Vice; Cold Water not Alcoholic Drinks or Medicines. It will indulge in no Gross Personalities and Insert no Quack or Immoral Advertisements, so common even in Religious Newspapers.

4. THE REVOLUTION proposes a new Commercial and Financial Policy. America no longer led by Europe. Gold like our Cotton and Corn for sale. Greenbacks for money. An American System of Finance. American Products and Labor Free. Foreign Manufacturers Prohibited. Open doors to Artisans and Immigrants. Atlantic and Pacific Oceans for American Steamships and Shipping; or American goods in American bottoms. New York the Financial Centre of the World. Wall Street emancipated from Bank of England, or American Cash for American Bills. The Credit Foncier and Credit Mobilier System, or Capital Mobilized to Resuscitate the South and our Mining Interests, and to People the Country from Ocean to Ocean, from Omaha to San Francisco. More organized Labor, more Cotton, more Gold and Silver Bullion to sell foreigners at the highest prices. Ten millions of Naturalized Citizens DEMAND A PENNY OCEAN POSTAGE, to Strengthen the Brotherhood of Labor; and if Congress Vote One Hundred and Twenty-five Millions for a Standing Army and Freedman's Bureau, cannot they spare One Million to Educate Europe and to keep bright the chain of acquaintance and friendship between those millions and their fatherland?

Send in your Subscription. THE REVOLUTION, published weekly, will be the Great Organ of the Age.

TERMS.—Two dollars a year, in advance. Ten names ($20) entitle the sender to one copy free.

ELIZABETH CADY STANTON, } EDS.
PARKER PILLSBURY, }

SUSAN B. ANTHONY,
Proprietor and Manager.
37 Park Row (Room 17), New York City,
To whom address all business letters.

KANSAS.

THE question of the enfranchisement of woman has already passed the court of moral discussion, and is now fairly ushered into the arena of politics, where it must remain a fixed element of debate, until party necessity shall compel its success.

With 9,000 votes in Kansas, one-third the entire vote, every politician must see that the friends of "woman's suffrage" hold the balance of power in that State to-day. And those 9,000 votes represent a principle deep in the hearts of the people, for this triumph was secured without money, without a press, without a party. With these instrumentalities now fast coming to us on all sides, the victory in Kansas is but the herald of greater victories in every State of the Union. Kansas already leads the world in her legislation for woman on questions of property, education, wages, marriage and divorce. Her best universities are open alike to boys and girls. In fact woman has a voice in the legislation of that State. She votes on all school questions and is eligible to the office of trustee. She has a voice in temperance too; no license is granted without the consent of a majority of the adult citizens, male and female, black and white. The consequence is, stone school houses are voted up in every part of the State, and rum voted down. Many of the ablest men in that State are champions of woman's cause. Governors, judges, lawyers and clergymen. Two-thirds of the press and pulpits advocate the idea, in spite of the opposition of politicians. The first Governor of Kansas, twice chosen to that office, Charles Robinson, went all through the State, speaking every day for two months in favor of woman's suffrage. In the organization of the State government, he proposed that the words "white male" should not be inserted in the Kansas constitution. All this shows that giving political rights to women is no new idea in that State. Who that has listened with tearful eyes to the deep experiences of those Kansas women, through the darkest hours of their history, does not feel that such bravery and self denial as they have shown alike in war and peace, have richly earned for them the crown of citizenship.

Opposed to this moral sentiment of the liberal minds of the State, many adverse influences were brought to bear through the entire campaign.

The action of the New York Constitutional Convention; the silence of eastern journals on the question; the opposition of abolitionists lost a demand for woman's suffrage should defeat negro suffrage; the hostility everywhere of black men themselves; some even stumping the State against woman's suffrage; the official action of both the leading parties in their conventions in Leavenworth against the proposition, with every organized Republican influ-

ence outside as well as inside the State, all combined might have made our vote comparatively a small one, had not George Francis Train gone into the State two weeks before the election and galvanized the Democrats into their duty, thus securing 9,000 votes for woman's suffrage. Some claim that we are indebted to the Republicans for this vote; but the fact that the most radical republican district, Douglass County, gave the largest vote against woman's suffrage, while Leavenworth, the Democratic district, gave the largest vote for it, fully settles that question.

In saying that Mr. Train helped to swell our vote takes nothing from the credit due all those who labored faithfully for months in that State. All praise to Olympia Brown, Lucy Stone, Susan B. Anthony, Henry B. Blackwell, and Judge Wood, who welcomed, for an idea, the hardships of travelling in a new State, fording streams, scaling rocky brinks, sleeping on the ground and eating hard tack, with the fatigue of constant speaking, in school-houses, barns, mills, depots and the open air; and especially, all praise to the glorious Hutchinson family—John, his son Henry and daughter Viola—who, with their own horses and carriage, made the entire circuit of the state, singing Woman's Suffrage into souls that logic could never penetrate. Having shared with them the hardships, with them I rejoice in our success.

E. C. S.

THE BALLOT—BREAD, VIRTUE, POWER.

THE REVOLUTION will contain a series of articles, beginning next week, to prove the power of the ballot in elevating the character and condition of woman. We shall show that the ballot will secure for woman equal place and equal wages in the world of work; that it will open to her the schools, colleges, professions and all the opportunities and advantages of life; that in her hand it will be a moral power to stay the tide of vice and crime and misery on every side. In the words of Bishop Simpson—

"We believe that the great vices in our large cities will never be conquered until the ballot is put in the hands of women. If the question of the danger of their sons being drawn away into drinking saloons was brought up, if the mothers had the power, they would close them; if the sisters had the power, and they saw their brothers going away to haunts of infamy, they would close those places. You may get men to tribe with purity, with virtue, with righteousness; but, thank God, the hearts of the women of our land—the mothers, wives and daughters—are too pure to make a compromise either with intemperance or licentiousness."

Thus, too, shall we purge our constitutions and statute laws from all invidious distinctions among the citizens of the States, and secure the same civil and moral code for man and woman. We will show the hundred thousand female teachers, and the millions of laboring women, that their complaints, petitions, strikes and protective unions are of no avail until they hold the ballot in their own hands; for it is the first step toward social, religious and political equality.

bust of Stone that would be displayed at the exposition. Stone was unable to attend the NAWSA's convention due to illness. She died shortly thereafter. She was seventy-five. She requested that she be cremated, a decision that was in line with her many other innovative ideas, as well as being ahead of its time. Her ashes are buried in Forest Hill Cemetery in Boston. Her daughter, Alice Stone Blackwell, published a biography of her mother in 1930.

The US Postal Service commemorated Lucy Stone by issuing a postage stamp in her honor on August 13, 1968, the 150th anniversary of her birth.

Stone's portrait was among a group of Massachusetts women leaders to be honored in the Massachusetts State House. Until 1999, only portraits of male leaders were on exhibit. Fortunately, a project initiated by the state legislature corrected this situation. Lucy Stone might have been most pleased by the establishment of the Lucy Stone Home Site, since she loved the natural beauty of the land surrounding her birthplace and was always inspired by it. It is now owned and managed by the Trustees of Reservations, a nonprofit land conservation and historic preservation organization dedicated to preserving natural and historic places in the Commonwealth of Massachusetts. The site includes sixty-one acres of forested land on the side of Coy's Hill in West Brookfield, Massachusetts. Although the farmhouse in which

Although she didn't live long enough to see women vote, Lucy Stone is recognized as a leader in the women's rights movement. A relief of Stone is displayed along with five other influential women in the Massachusetts state house.

Stone was born and married burned to the ground in 1950, its ruins are at the center of the property.

Stone has not received the recognition that she deserved for the work she contributed to the suffrage movement. In part, that is due to the feud between Stone and Stanton and Anthony over the Fifteenth Amendment issue. When Susan B. Anthony, Elizabeth Cady Stanton, and others wrote the *History of Woman Suffrage,* Stone's work and accomplishments were minimized. Since the book was considered to be the standard for a scholarly resource on the American suffrage movement for much of the twentieth century, many of Stone's accomplishments and achievements have been overlooked by scholars.

Stone's tireless and persuasive speaking and organizing moved the cause of woman's rights forward for decades, and her work remains a model for woman's rights advocacy today, especially in the area of equal pay for equal work. The first, and for years the only advocate for the rights of women, she is justly referred to as "the morning star of the women's rights movement."

CHAPTER FIVE

THE LEGACY

The legacy that Matilda Joslyn Gage, Julia Ward Howe, Lucretia Mott, and Lucy Stone left to the women of today, and to all the people of the world, is hard to calculate. Because of them, and the many others who fought for women's rights and freedom, American women won the right to vote, the right to own property, the right to earn and manage their own money, the right of equal standing before the law, the right to access the courts for redress of grievances, the right to admission to institutions of higher learning, the right to seek and hold public office, the right to enter into and practice all

The fight taken on by Matilda Gage, Julia Howe, Lucretia Mott, and Lucy Stone was only the beginning. Armed with the vote and increasing political power, women in the 1960s and 1970s engaged in a new women's liberation movement.

professions, and so many more freedoms. Without the dedication of these women, life for women today would probably be very similar to life in the nineteenth century.

It is easy for us to take these rights for granted. But these liberties were hard won, and many still remain to be fulfilled. One of the most basic is safety from physical violence. If we think about the story in this book describing the right of a man in the nineteenth century to beat his wife, we can see that there is still domestic violence and spousal abuse to overcome. Or if we think about the lack of equal pay that women like Lucy Stone and Lucretia Mott encountered, we realize that many women face that same discrimination today. It is estimated that in the United States, women on average make $0.79 for every $1.00 earned by men.[1]

If these women's rights leaders were here today, looking at our nation and our world, what would they think? They would be very happy to

Where once US women weren't allowed to speak in public or cast a vote, they are now represented in important government positions, as this photo of the Democratic women of the 114th Congress shows.

see women running for president in both major
political parties. They would be delighted to
see women occupying professions in business,
technology, and science. They would be glad to
see women holding positions of organizational
leadership. They would applaud women having the
right to serve in combat roles in the armed forces,
although they would probably be distressed that
anyone has to go to war. They would probably support rights for lesbian and transgendered women.
They would be pleased to see women in the arts
and entertainment sectors occupying leadership
roles. They would be happy to see so many women
entrepreneurs.

But what conditions would make them urge us
all to continue the fight for women's rights? They
would probably be sad to see that only about one-
third of both men and women describe themselves
as regular voters,[2] and they would push us to get
out the vote. They would urge us to pass the Equal
Rights Amendment (ERA) to the Constitution.
They would probably say that there is still ignorance,
defensiveness, and misogyny toward women
that is preventing them from fulfilling their role in
society. They would say that a woman should be
paid equally for equal work. They would ask why,
if women are 50 percent of the population, they
aren't 50 percent of the Congress.

If these women looked beyond our own country
(and these women heroes would look) at the

condition of women around the world, they would see much work to be done. They, like Frederick Douglass, would ask, why do we waste 50 percent of our people power by not educating and empowering women to do the work of humanity?

These great suffrage leaders would have advocated for health care for women in poor countries; for their legal, social, economic, and political rights; for education for girls; for protecting their physical safety; and for the encouragement and mentoring that would bring them into roles of leadership.

Our women's suffrage leaders ask us to do this work—and more. They would encourage us to envision, to dream, to work—and to never, ever give up.

CHAPTER NOTES

INTRODUCTION. BEFORE SUFFRAGE

1. Elizabeth Frost and Kathryn Cullen-DuPont, *Women's Suffrage in America: An Eyewitness History* (New York: Facts on File, Inc., 1992), p. 3.
2. *Alice Stone Blackwell, Lucy Stone: Pioneer of Woman's Rights* (Boston: Little, Brown, and Company, 1930), p. 6.

CHAPTER 1. MATILDA JOSLYN GAGE

1. Dr. Sally Roesch Wagner, "The Underground Railroad Room," the Matilda Joslyn Gage Foundation, http://www.matildajoslyngage org/gage-home/underground-railroad-room/ Underground railroad room (December 4, 2015).
2. Ibid.
3. Ellen Carol Dubois, *Feminism and Suffrage: The Emergence of an Independent Women's Movement in America 1848–1869* (Ithaca and London: Cornell University Press, 1978), pp. 24–25.
4. "Matilda Joslyn Gage," n.d., http://biography .yourdictionary.com/matilda-joslyn-gage (December 9, 2015).
5. Ibid.
6. "Women's Rights Room," the Matilda Joslyn Gage Foundation, http://www.matildajoslyngage

.org/gage-home/womens-rights-room/ (December 4, 2015).

7. Ibid.

8. Matilda Joslyn Gage, *Woman, Church and State* (New York: The Truth Seeker Company, 1893) (Scanned at Sacred-texts.com, March–April 2002. John Bruno Hare, Redactor), pp. 16–18.

9. Ibid., p. 243.

10. Dr. Melinda Grube, "The Religious Freedom Room," the Matilda Joslyn Gage Foundation, http://www.matildajoslyngage.org/gage-home/religious -freedom-room/ (December 4, 2015).

11. "Haudenoseunee Room," the Matilda Joslyn Gage Foundation, http://www.matildajoslyn -gage.org/gage-home/Haudenosaunee-room/ (December 4, 2015).

12. Dr. Sally Roesch Wagner, "Family Parlor and Oz Room," the Matilda Joslyn Gage Foundation, http://www.matildajoslyngage.org/gage-home/baumoz -family-room/ (December 4, 2015).

13. "Matilda Joslyn Gage Gravesite," the Free Thought Trail, http://www.freethought-trail.org/site (December 8, 2015).

14. Women in Science, https://womenscience .wordpress.com/gender-stereotypes/matilda -effect/ (December 8, 2015).

15. The Matilda Joslyn Gage Foundation, http://www.matildajoslyngage.org/tea-with-gloria -steinem-dec-4-2011/ (December 8, 2015).

CHAPTER 2. JULIA WARD HOWE

1. Jone Johnson Lewis, "Julia Ward Howe Early Years," About Education, http://womenshistory.about.com/od/howejuliaward/a/julia_ward_howe_1_early (November 30, 2015).
2. Laura E. Richards and Maud Howe Elliott, *Julia Ward Howe 1819–1910* (Boston and New York: Houghton Mifflin Company, 1925), p. 153.
3. Ibid., p. 198.
4. Ibid., p. 197.
5. Ibid., p. 197.

CHAPTER 3. LUCRETIA COFFIN MOTT

1. Margaret Hope Bacon, *Valiant Friend: The Life of Lucretia Mott* (Walker and Company, New York, 1980), p. 10.
2. Ibid., p. 44.
3. Ibid., p. 77.
4. Nancy C. Unger, "Mott, Lucretia Coffin," American National Biography Online, Feb. 2000, http://www.anb.org/articles/15/15 (December 8, 2015).
5. Margaret Hope Bacon, *Valiant Friend: The Life of Lucretia Mott*, p. 105
6. Ibid., p.116.

CHAPTER 4. LUCY STONE

1. Alice Stone Blackwell, *Lucy Stone: Pioneer of Woman's Rights* (Boston: Little, Brown, and Company, 1930), p. 9.
2. Ibid., p. 3.
3. Biography.com Editors, "Mary Lyon Biography," http://www.biography.com/people/mary -lyon-9389865 (November 29, 2015).
4. Alice Stone Blackwell, *Lucy Stone: Pioneer of Woman's Rights,* p. 21.
5. Ibid., p. 90.

CHAPTER 5: THE LEGACY

1. "Pay Equity and Discrimination," http://www .iwpr.org/initiatives/pay-equity-and-discrimination (December 13, 2015).
2. "Who Votes, Who Doesn't, And Why," October 18, 2006, http://www.people-press.org/2006/10/18/ who-votes-who-doesnt-and-why/ (December 13, 2015).

GLOSSARY

abolition Elimination of the institution of slavery.

asylum A place that offers shelter and help to mentally ill people.

enfranchisement To make a citizen, especially including the right to vote.

entrepreneur One who creates and runs a successful business.

Equal Rights Amendment An effort to guarantee civil rights for women in the United States.

franchise The right to vote.

free state A state where slavery is illegal.

Fugitive Slave Law A law that enforced the return of runaway slaves to their masters.

glass ceiling An unofficial barrier to professional advancement for women.

legacy Something of value left to others.

lynching The mob killing of a person without a trial.

matriarchy A group or society ruled by a woman or women.

matrilineal Based on a relationship with the mother or the mother's family.

patriarchy A group or society ruled by a man or men.

physiology Part of the science of biology.

redress of grievances The right to seek

something from government without fear.

sanction To give permission, or accept a belief or behavior.

spinster An unmarried woman of an age at which she is not expected to marry.

suffrage The right to vote.

suffragette A female who seeks the right to vote for women; sometimes a demeaning term.

suffragist A person who seeks the right to vote for women.

theology The study of God and religion.

FURTHER READING

BOOKS

Benoit, Peter. *Women's Right to Vote*. New York: Children's Press, 2014.

Carson, Mary Kay, and Robert Hunt. *Why Couldn't Susan B. Anthony Vote?: And Other Questions About Women's Suffrage*. New York: Sterling Children's Books, 2015.

Guillain, Charlotte. *Stories of Women's Suffrage*. Chicago: Heinemann Raintree, 2015.

Jones, Elizabeth McDavid. *Secrets on 26th Street*. New York: Open Road Media, 2014.

Mead, Maggie, and Siri Weber Feeney. *Suffrage Sisters: The Fight for Liberty*. South Egremont, MA: Red Chair Press, 2015.

Metz, Lorijo. *The Women's Suffrage Movement*. New York: PowerKids Press, 2013.

Nardo, Don. *The Split History of the Women's Suffrage Movement: A Perspectives Flip Book*. North Mankato, MN: Compass Point Books, 2014.

Nash, Carol Rust. *Women Winning the Right to Vote in United States History*. Berkeley Heights, NJ: Enslow Publishers, Inc., 2014.

Peppas, Lynn. *Women's Suffrage*. St. Catherine's, ON: Crabtree Publishing Co., 2015.

WEBSITES

National Woman's History Museum

www.nwhm.org/education-resources
The website provides a wealth of historical information on women through the ages. It also provides an excellent and extensive list of biographies of women who have achieved in a variety of areas.

Women's Rights National Historical Park, National Parks Service

www.nps.gov/wori/learn/historyculture/index.htm
The Women's Rights National Historical Park is located in Seneca Falls, New York, and is a wonderful place to visit to get the feel of what happened in the early years of the women's suffrage movement. The website itself offers descriptions of some of the historic locations in the area, as well as background information on women suffrage leaders and women leaders today.

INDEX

A

abolitionists, 18, 22, 50, 70, 72–73, 75, 77, 94

African Americans, 16–17, 30, 37, 72, 77, 94, 102

alcohol/alcohol abuse, 15, 30. See also Prohibition, Temperance

American Academy of Arts and Letters, 61

American Anti–Slavery Society, 22, 70, 97

American Equal Rights Association, 82–83, 102

American Woman Suffrage Association (AWSA), 54, 59, 83, 103, 105

Anthony, Susan B., 22–24, 26, 28–29, 31, 57–58, 82–83, 85, 95, 99–103, 108

antirape laws, 30

antislavery, 72
   advocates, 24, 50, 73
   beliefs, 23, 69

Association for the Advancement of Women, 59

Astor, Emily, 44

B

"Battle Hymn of the Republic, The," 51, 53, 61–62

Baum, L. Frank, 38–39

Baum, Maud, 38–39

Bible, 9, 13, 27–28, 98

Blackwell, Alice Stone, 100, 107

Blackwell, Elizabeth, 99

Blackwell, Emily, 99

Blackwell, Henry, 99

black women, 16–17, 73. See also African Americans

Blatch, Harriot Stanton, 105

"Bloody Kansas," 50

Bloomer, Amelia, 95

Brown, John, 50

C

Calhoun, John C., 78

Canada, 46, 50, 75, 99, 105

careers, for women, 11, 14, 19, 39, 97

child abuse, 30, 35

Christian church/ Christianity, 27, 31, 34, 40

church, 6, 9, 14, 16, 24, 27, 29–32, 34, 40, 46, 55, 90–91, 94, 97, 99

Civil War, 23, 50, 53, 56, 70, 82, 101

"classical" education, 13–14

clothing, 8–10, 66, 95

clubs, 53–55

Coffin, Anna Folger, 63, 65, 68, 78

Coffin, Martha, 69

Coffin, Thomas, Jr., 63, 65

Commentator, 50

Crandall, Prudence, 17

D

Declaration of Sentiments, 80

Declaration of the Rights of Women, 28

"Discourse on Women," (1850), 82

Dix, Dorothea, 46

domestic
   life, 4, 9, 11
   violence, 48, 112

Douglass, Frederick, 58, 82, 115

E

economics, 24, 27, 38, 115
education, of women, 8, 13–14, 16, 19–22, 30, 38, 59, 65, 85, 90–91, 93–97, 100, 115
Eighteenth Amendment, 30
enslaved women, 16–18
equal
  pay, 19, 109, 112
  rights, 22, 57, 82, 101–102, 114
Equal Rights Amendment (ERA), 114
Europe, 32, 47, 56

F

Fifteenth Amendment, 22, 57, 101–103, 108
First Anti-Slavery Convention of American Women (1837), 72
First National Women's Rights Convention (1850), 99

Foster, Abby Kelley, 20, 22, 70, 91, 105
Foster, Stephen, 22, 97
Fourteenth Amendment, 57, 83, 101
Free Religious Association, 55
Fugitive Slave Act, 23, 50, 94

G

Gage, Henry H., 23, 25
Gage, Matilda Joslyn, 19, 85, 110
  abolition activities, 23–24
  birth, 20
  childhood, 20
  children, 38–39
  education, 20, 22
  foundation, 40–41
  legacy of, 39–41
  L. Frank Baum friendship, 38–39
  marriage, 23, 35
  Native Americans and, 35–37
  religion, 30–31
  violence against women, 31–35
  women's rights activism, 24, 26–29
Garrison, William Lloyd, 22, 58, 70, 72, 82, 90, 94, 97

General Federation of Women's Clubs, 55
Green, Catherine Littlefield, 28
Grimké, Angelina, 18, 22, 70, 72–73, 91, 93
Grimké, Sarah, 18, 72, 91, 95

H

Harpers Ferry, 50
Haudenosaunee Confederacy, 35
health care, 19, 115
History of Woman Suffrage, 28–29, 40, 108–109
Howe, Julia Ward, 19, 83, 103, 110
  "Battle Hymn of the Republic, The," 51, 53, 61
  birth, 42
  childhood, 42
  children, 47–48
  clubs, 53–55
  death, 62
  education, 42, 44
  later years, and honors, 61–62
  marriage, 44–49
  religion, and pacifism, 55–56
  travel, 47–48

war work, 50–51, 53
women's suffrage,
56–59
writing, 48–51, 53
Howe, Samuel Gridley,
44–49
Hutchinson, Ann, 6

I

Iroquois Nation, 16, 32,
35–36

J

Joslyn, Helen Leslie, 20
Joslyn, Hezekiah, 20
jury duty, 9

K

King, Martin Luther, Jr.,
86

L

legal rights
of men, 4, 6–8,
10–11, 13–15,
48–49, 54, 100
of women, 8–11, 15,
24, 47, 115
"Legal Rights of
Mothers to Their
Children, The," 103
lesbian, and transgen-
dered women, 114

Liberal Thinker, 34
Liberator, 58, 70, 89,
97
Lincoln, Abraham, 51
Lucretia Mott Award,
86
lynching, 30
Lyon, Mary, 90–91

M

marriage, 8, 11, 36
Massachusetts Woman
Suffrage
Association, 54
matriarchate, or mother
rule, 32, 39–40
matrilineal culture, 16
Middle Passage, 65
misogynistic attitude,
34, 114
Mohawk, 35, 37
Mother's Day holiday,
56
Mott, James, Jr.,
66–69, 74, 80, 82
Mott, James, Sr., 66
Mott, Lucretia Coffin,
19, 110, 112
abolition, 70, 72–74,
77–78
birth, 63
childhood, 63, 65–66
children, 68–69
death, 83
education, 65–67

honors, and legacy,
83, 85–86
marriage, 67–69
Seneca Falls, 79–80,
82–83
travels, 74, 77–78
women's rights, 70,
72–74, 77–80,
82–83, 85–86
Mount Holyoke
Seminary, 90–91
Ms. magazine, 38

N

National American
Woman Suffrage
Association
(NAWSA), 105, 107
National Citizen and
Ballot Box, 28, 37
National Woman
Suffrage
Association
(NWSA), 26,
28–29, 31, 58–59,
83, 103, 105
National Women's
Political Caucus, 38
Native Americans,
35–37, 39. *See
also specific tribes*
New England Suffrage
Association, 54
New England Woman's
Club, 54-55

ragists, 16, 19, 22,
  26, 34, 42, 57, 83,
  95, 105
nner, Charles, 23

perance, 15–16,
  23, 30–31, 85
ngular Trade, 65
Female Seminary,
  14
r, John, 77–78

derground Railroad,
  20, 23, 75, 93
iversal Peace Union,
  83
Capitol, 85–86
Congress, 94, 101,
  114
Constitution,
  30–31, 57, 59, 83,
  94, 114
Postal Service,
  stamps, 62, 107
Sanitary
  Commission, 51

torian society, 35
ence, against
  women, 17, 31–35,

48. *See also*
  Domestic violence,
  Physical abuse
Virginia Woman
  Suffrage
  Association, 28
voters, 10, 29, 50, 114
voting rights, 9–10, 16,
  26, 29–30, 37, 40,
  58, 82–83, 85, 91,
  101–103, 105,
  110, 114

W

Wagner, Sally Roesch,
  40
Wakefield, Priscilla,
  65–66
Ward, Julia, 42
Ward, Sam, 44
Ward, Samuel III, 42
Wells, Ida B., 30
Whitney, Ann, 105, 107
Whitney, Eli, 28
"Who Planned the
  Tennessee
  Campaign of
  1862?" (1880), 28
widows, 11, 14, 53
Willard, Emma, 14
Willard, Frances, 30–31
"wise women," 32
witch burning, 32–34
"Woman as Inventor"
  (1870), 28

*Woman, Church, and
  State* (1893),
  31–32
Woman's Bible, The, 28
Woman's Christian
  Temperance Union
  (WCTU), 30–31
Woman's Journal
  (AWSA), 59, 103
"Woman's Rights
  Catechism" (1871),
  28
Women's Action
  Alliance, 38
Women's Media Center,
  38
Women's National
  Liberal Union
  (WNLU), 29,
  34–35
Women's Political
  Caucus, 38
Women's Rights
  National
  Convention (1852),
  24
*Wonderful Wizard of
  Oz*, 38–39
World's Anti–Slavery
  Convention (1840),
  74, 77

New England Woman
Suffrage
Association, 102
New Jersey Woman
Suffrage
Association, 102
New York Woman
Suffrage
Association, 28–29
Nineteenth
Amendment, 30
nonresistance, 30
nonviolence, 70

O

Oberlin College,
93–96, 100
Oneida, 35
Onondaga, 35
oppression, of women,
24, 26
orphans, 14, 53

P

pacifism, 55–56
Parker, Theodore,
46–47, 50
patriarchate, or male
rule, 24, 32, 34
Pennsylvania Peace
Society, 83
Philadelphia Female
Anti–Slavery
Society, 72

physical abuse, 6, 112,
115. See also
Domestic violence,
Violence against
women
politics, 22, 29–31
prohibition, 15–16, 30,
105
property rights, 9, 17,
32, 35, 59, 85,
105, 110
Puritan women, 6

Q

Quakers (Society of
Friends), 17, 22,
65–70, 78, 80, 83

R

Reconstruction, 101
religion, 6, 14, 31, 34,
40, 42, 44–45,
54–56, 68
Revolution (NWSA), 103
"rule of thumb," 6
runaway slaves, 23, 46,
50, 75, 93

S

Seneca, 35
Seneca Falls, 26,
79–80, 82–83,
123

sexual
single
slavery,
39,
72,
94
Smith, G
spinster
Stanton
Cad
28–
79–
95,
108
Steinem
86
Stone, L
53–
70, 8
abolitic
birth, 8
childhc
childre
death,
educat
93
marriag
99
Oberlin
93
public s
96
recogni
10
suffrage
10

su

Su

T

ter

Tri
Tro

Ty

U

Ur

Ur

U:
U

U

U

U

V

V
vi